Vajragupta has written an excellent synopsis of the history of an important Buddhist movement. This is of interest to all of us who are concerned with the arrival of Buddhism in the West and the vicissitudes of Buddhist movements through periods of social change over the past half century: the triumphs and disasters, the glory and the tears, the pioneering spirit and the dilemmas of success and failure – it is all set out here in an easy to digest narrative that I found, by turns, informative, nostalgic, encouraging, and challenging. This helps us to gain perspective and to see our way forward with greater clarity.

David Brazier; author and head of the Amida-shu

The Triratna Story is a courageous and important book. Written by a serious adherent, and commissioned by the Triratna Community itself, it defies all expectations to tell the brilliant, troubled, and inspiring history of this unique Western Buddhist movement with a thoroughness and honesty that, frankly, would not have been possible had it been written by an outsider. This is a valuable and instructive text for anyone interested in looking beyond the idealism of the Buddhist teachings to what actually happens when Buddhism becomes real in the modern world.

Zoketsu Norman Fischer; poet, author and founder of the Everyday Zen Foundation

Published by
Windhorse Publications Ltd.
169 Mill Road
Cambridge CB1 3AN, UK
email: info@windhorsepublications.com
www.windhorsepublications.com

Cover design by Vidyadaka
Printed by Bell & Bain Ltd., Glasgow

Cover credits::
Above title (clockwise from top left):
1 Ordination at Padmaloka; from Sangharakshita's collection, held by ClearVision;
2 Renovating the London Buddhist Centre, courtesy London Buddhist Centre archive;
3 Young meditators, circa 1970, courtesy London Buddhist Centre archive; 4 Lokamitra
and Ambedkar shrine, 1980 © FWBO Photos; 5 Sangharakshita, early 1970s, Clear
Vision; 6 Exterior London Buddhist Centre, courtesy London Buddhist Centre archive;
7 Chintamani with Buddha sculpture, courtesy London Buddhist Centre.
Below title (clockwise from top left):
1 Children making offerings © FWBO Photos; 2 Aloka with mural, London Buddhist
Centre © FWBO Photos; 3 Sangharakshita portrait © Alokavira/Timm Sonnenschein;
4 People meditating with Buddha rupa © Alokavira/Timm Sonnenschein; 5 Western
Buddhist Order Convention Stupa, 2007 © FWBO Photos; 6 Stupa in the warehouse
of Windhorse Evolution, Cambridge © FWBO Photos; 7 TBMSG Retreat, India ©
FWBO Photos; 8 Golden shrine, London Buddhist Centre © FWBO Photos;
9 Guhyaloka Ordination Centre, Spain.

British Library Cataloguing in Publication Data:
A catalogue record for this book is available from the British Library

ISBN: 9781 899579 92 1

The Triratna Story

Behind the Scenes of a
New Buddhist Movement

by

Vajragupta

Windhorse Publications

You learn what it is you are trying to do
in the process of trying to do it.

Sangharakshita
Peace is a Fire*

* Windhorse Publications 1995, p.39

Contents

Acknowledgements

I would like to thank the many people who sent me stories and anecdotes for this project. I felt honoured to receive them. All of them, even the ones that I couldn't fit into the book, gave me inspiration and encouragement.

Many thanks to those who were willing to be interviewed: Dhammaloka, Dharmamati, Karunadipa, Lokamdhara, Manjunatha, Nagabodhi, Nityabandhu, Rupavati, Sona, Suvarnaprabha, Vajradhara, and Vidyamala. I'm also grateful to Vaddhaka for letting me stay in his flat during the autumn of 2008, and to Matthew Hart for allowing me to stay in his summerhouse on the banks of the Severn.

The feedback from those who read an early draft of the book was very helpful, particularly from Kalyacitta, Vaddhaka, and Lokabandhu (a colleague in the Triratna Development Team who also took time to dig out statistics and snippets of information from the memory banks of his computer). Roy Peters gave invaluable help with sourcing the photos.

I'd especially like to thank Siddhisambhava (another colleague in the Development Team), whose comments and suggestions have significantly improved the text. She also gave me numerous tips about useful books to read, or people to talk to.

Caroline Jestaz at Windhorse Publications gave me much advice and support, as did two of their trustees, Sagaraghosa and Vajrapushpa. I'm grateful to Maitripushpa who generously gave her time to edit the book.

I'd also like to acknowledge my indebtedness to Subhuti and Vishvapani. They've written many articles and papers (often quoted in the text) that helped me make sense of the development of the FWBO, especially its last ten years.

Lastly, thank you, Sangharakshita, for commenting on the manuscript, and, most of all, for having the courage to start a new Buddhist movement for the West. Without you, there would be no story to tell in the first place.

About the author

Vajragupta was born as Richard Staunton in 1968 and grew up in London. He studied social science at university and first came into contact with Buddhism at the Birmingham Buddhist Centre (a centre of the Friends of the Western Buddhist Order) in the early 1990s. He was ordained in 1994 and given the name Vajragupta which means 'secret, or hidden, diamond-like truth'. He was director of the Birmingham Buddhist Centre from 1997 to 2005, and is now director of the FWBO Development Team – working for a collective of 50 FWBO centres and projects across Europe. He currently lives in Worcester, England where he teaches Buddhism and meditation, enjoys walking and wildlife, reading, poetry, and travelling over to nearby Stratford to watch productions of Shakespeare plays. His first book, published in 2007 by Windhorse Publications, was *Buddhism: Tools for Living Your Life*.

Foreword: From the FWBO to Triratna Buddhist Community

When I wrote this book, I was writing a history of a Buddhist movement known as the 'Friends of the Western Buddhist Order' (FWBO for short). However, just weeks before the book went to press, Sangharakshita – founder of the FWBO – proposed that it should change its name to 'Triratna Buddhist Community'. After a couple of months of discussion and debate, it was decided that this name change would go ahead. This suggested change, which was quite sudden and unexpected, presented me and the publishers of the book with a problem. It looks very likely that the name change proposal will be accepted and that in a year or so, people contacting this movement will hear much more about 'Triratna Buddhist Community' than the 'FWBO'.

So, what to do about the book? Our working title was *The Story of the FWBO* and on almost every page the movement is referred to by that name. Would that quickly seem strange and outdated? On the other hand, it seemed artificial to go through the text of the book and replace every mention of 'FWBO' with the new name. After all, where the book talks about the movement in the 1970s or 1980s, 'FWBO' was what it was known as at that time. We have therefore decided to keep the text pretty much the same, apart from telling the story of the name change right at the end. This book is the story of a movement founded as the 'Friends of the Western Buddhist Order', but now known as the 'Triratna Buddhist Community'. In a way, it's quite neat: the book covers a complete phase in the movement's history, that period of time when it was known as the 'FWBO', and shows the origins and evolution of that which will grow into the future as the Triratna Buddhist Community.

Why has the name been changed? For a full explanation of the reasons, please see the postscript of the book. But, in brief, there was a need to have a name that could be used all over the world. 'Friends of the Western Buddhist Order' had been a good name in the West, but it was obviously not appropriate in India, which is where the movement is growing fastest. In India the movement has always been known as "Trailokya Bauddha Mahasangha Sahayaka Gana" (TBMSG) – the 'Association of Helpers of the Spiritual Community of the Three Worlds'. The name "Western" would be unsuitable elsewhere too, such as in the Chinese speaking world.

So there was a desire for one name that united the movement worldwide, and Sangharakshita's suggestion was based round the sanskrit word "Triratna". This means "Three Jewels" which are the three most precious ideals of Buddhism. Firstly there is the Buddha-jewel – the ideal of Enlightenment and the developing of Wisdom and Compassion which Buddhism teaches is the deepest potential of us all. Secondly, there is the Dharma-jewel: the teachings and practices that help us move towards Enlightenment. Thirdly, there is the Sangha-jewel: the community of those who share those ideals and practices and who are committed to helping each other on the path.

By basing the name of the movement around the word "Triratna", Sangharakshita was emphasising the importance of these three ideals, and the need for Buddhism to renew itself in the modern world by going back to the essential teachings and principles.

The Triratna Chairs Assembly

This book was commissioned and partly funded by the Triratna Chairs' Assembly, a collective of 50 Chairs and Directors of Triratna Buddhist Community projects. These include urban centres, several retreat centres, and other pan-movement projects such as Free Buddhist Audio and Clear Vision. Each Triratna centre and project is run independently. At the same time, the Assembly works together to ensure the unity and vitality of the Triratna Buddhist Community in Europe and beyond.

The Triratna Chairs Assembly Fund helps many things happen. It currently employs three Order members (the Triratna Development Team) to carry out the decisions of the Assembly, such as organising Triratna international retreats. It initiates and funds movement-wide resources such as the new Dharma training course for Mitras, and the forthcoming redesigned Triratna Buddhist Community website.

There are so many more things we could do with greater resources. For example, we'd like to be able to help pioneers founding Buddhist centres in new countries and locations, fund translations of Dharma books into new languages, produce teaching resources, get the Buddha's message onto the Internet where so many more people, especially young people, might come across it. We hope you'll be excited and inspired to donate to the Assembly Fund. If you'd like to discuss a one-off or regular donation, or leaving the Assembly Fund a gift in your will, please contact Vajragupta, Director of the Triratna Development Team (vajragupta@fwbo.org).

Preface

In the early 1990s, as a young man of 22, I started attending the Birmingham Buddhist Centre, part of the Friends of the Western Buddhist Order (FWBO). This was, I discovered, a new Buddhist movement for the West, started by an Englishman who as a young man had travelled to India and been ordained as a Buddhist monk, receiving the name Sangharakshita. In the mid-1960s he'd returned to the West, where there was a wave of enthusiasm for things mystical and Eastern. Riding that wave, he founded the FWBO in 1968. He was an inspired and brilliant teacher and the FWBO grew rapidly, opening centres in many parts of the world.

In Birmingham, there was a thriving and friendly centre with a busy programme of classes, retreats, and festivals. There was also a residential community and a 'right livelihood business' just getting off the ground. It felt like the chance to get involved in an exciting adventure, helping to establish something new. Here was a group of people living a radically alternative way of life. I quickly threw myself in.

I learned that some people in the FWBO became ordained into the Western Buddhist Order (WBO). This didn't entail becoming a monk, but it did mean 'going for refuge' – putting the ideals of the Buddha, Dharma (the Buddha's teachings), and Sangha (the spiritual community) right at the centre of your life. Many Order members worked for the FWBO, teaching classes and running the activities of the Buddhist centre. I knew that was what I wanted to do and I asked to be ordained. After an unhappy period at university, where I'd felt lost and unsure of my direction,

I'd found something that had meaning and value. I wanted to give myself to it wholeheartedly, and my Buddhist life took off quickly. I was ordained in 1994, and by late 1997 I'd become the Chair of the Birmingham Buddhist Centre.

It was at this time that the *Guardian* – a UK national newspaper – ran a highly critical piece on the FWBO. The events the paper reported on had happened many years before, in the relatively early days of the FWBO. Yet, based on those events, the newspaper article claimed the FWBO was a cult, and that it distorted Buddhist teachings, was 'anti-family', and promoted homosexuality. The article appeared on a Monday. On Tuesday evening, we held the main weekly class at the Birmingham Buddhist Centre. I'd been Chair of the Buddhist Centre for only three weeks, and I went along to the class with some trepidation.

Some people were shocked and angered by what they'd read, but I was surprised by the extent to which most didn't take it that seriously. Their response was similar to mine; the newspaper piece seemed oversensationalized and what it described was not remotely like our experience of being involved in the FWBO.

However, after that article came more scandal on the Internet, where some Order members began revealing their unhappiness about aspects of the FWBO's past. For people like me and my friends at the Birmingham Centre, this was more disturbing. It was possible to dismiss criticism that came from outside, and that seemed so extreme and one-sided. If, however, members of your own community said that some of it was true, that was much more troubling. Even though my friends and I weren't personally involved in the FWBO during the time in question, it still reflected on us and the organization we were involved in. The *Guardian* article began a period of intense self-questioning and soul-searching for many involved in the FWBO.

Ten years later, I'd moved on from the Birmingham Buddhist Centre and was now working for the European FWBO Chairs

Assembly – a collective of chairs and directors of about 50 FWBO centres and projects from across Europe. In 2007, as part of its work maintaining an overview of the FWBO, the assembly came up with six 'strategic priorities'. One of these was to: 'Tell the story of our "troubles" – truthfully, in a way that fosters understanding and confidence.'

The website containing criticisms of the FWBO was still online, and scored a high ranking if you typed 'FWBO' into a search engine. People considering attending an FWBO centre, or those who were early in their involvement at one, were sure to come across the material and might easily be put off the FWBO and even the Buddha's teaching. It was impossible to tell exactly how many were deterred in this way, though I knew from my involvement in centre work that some people were. We needed to have a much better response to these criticisms and the questions they brought up.

It also seemed to me that, as a community, we had stopped telling our story during that period of questioning. In the early days, people talked eagerly about the FWBO and its role in bringing Buddhism to the West. After the *Guardian* article, that story didn't quite ring true any more. The reality was rather more complex and difficult. It was also harder to talk meaningfully and accurately about the FWBO because it was getting bigger, more geographically spread, more diverse as a community. As a consequence of this, the FWBO Newsreel, a twice-yearly video that reported and reflected on the FWBO, had ceased production in 2003. *Dharma Life* magazine, another important channel of communication about the FWBO, also closed down two years later due to unrelated economic factors. The overall result was that we were doing much less to tell people in the FWBO about ourselves, what we stood for, what we'd learned in 40 years of bringing Buddhism to the West. How would those involved at local FWBO centres come to realize that they were part of this much bigger, worldwide movement? We needed to learn how to talk about ourselves – and our history – again.

The European FWBO Chairs Assembly eventually tasked me with that 'strategic priority' and the result is this book – an attempt to tell our story anew.

⚬

It's a story of sheer audacity – a Buddhist teacher starting from scratch, working with a group of young people who had only the vaguest ideas about the Dharma. He told them they were going to bring Buddhism to the West – in a way that had never been attempted before.

It's the story of a circle of friends dreaming a dream, and working to make it a reality. They were, by necessity, finding out what it was they were trying to do as they went along. It's the nitty-gritty story of how a community evolves. It's a tale of idealism and naivety, growth and growing pains, hard work and burnout, friendship and fallout. It's a celebration of how so much was achieved in so short a time, and a reflection on the mistakes made, and lessons learned.

This book attempts to 'take stock' of the first 40 years of the FWBO. It draws together material from many sources into one narrative. A community needs to tell – and retell – its story in this way. It is one means by which a community learns about itself, and grows into the future. As the novelist Ursula Le Guin has noted:

> The story – from *Rumpelstiltskin* to *War and Peace* – is one of the basic tools invented by the human mind, for the purpose of gaining understanding. There have been great societies that did not use the wheel, but there have been no societies that did not tell stories.[1]

Of course, there will be as many versions of this story as there are people to tell it. There is a wide range of views and experiences of the topics discussed in this book. What authority do I have to present a 'history of the FWBO'?

As I've said, I am a member of the Western Buddhist Order; I don't claim to be a neutral, outside observer. I've spent many years teaching at a public Buddhist centre and seeing how people new to the FWBO tend to perceive it. However, having been ordained in the mid-1990s, I belong to the generation that came after Sangharakshita and the early pioneers had established the FWBO. As a consequence, I feel I've been involved enough with the FWBO to understand what really went on, but I am also 'second generation' enough to be able to stand back and review. I'm not interested in doing either a hagiography of the FWBO or a hatchet job. I want to write with empathy for all involved. I feel a strong sense of gratitude to those who worked so hard to establish the FWBO, so that people like myself could hear the teachings of the Buddha communicated in a modern form.

The story is roughly in chronological order, though some of the middle chapters also jump back and forth in time in order to explore a particular theme in more detail: Chapter 5 discusses work and lifestyle, Chapter 6 explores how the FWBO developed men's and women's wings, Chapter 7 is about the international and cultural diversity of the FWBO, and Chapter 8 relates the history of the Order and ordination training processes.

It is written primarily for an FWBO audience rather than for members of the WBO, who have had their own forums in which to discuss the kinds of issues covered here. My brief was to write something short and easily readable. It has ended up being just over 1,000 words for each of the 42 years of the FWBO's history. There are inevitable limitations in trying to cover so much ground in so short a space. Many stories have been left out, countless acts of generosity not celebrated, numerous issues dealt with only very briefly.

I'm also aware that my experience of the FWBO has largely been in the UK, and that probably is reflected in the story I tell. I'm especially conscious that the largest numbers of people involved in our movement are in India, and yet that aspect of the movement is covered in just one chapter of the book (Chapter 4). This history needs to be seen as an attempt to give a concise and accessible picture of the FWBO, but one that focuses mainly on its development in the West.

In the endnotes to the text, you'll find references to books, magazine articles, and websites where you can learn more about the topics discussed. Though I am responsible for the text, and the opinions expressed and conclusions reached are mine, the book has been written with the help and cooperation of many people, including Sangharakshita.

Vajragupta, October 2009

1
Counterculture

It's a spring evening in central London in 1967. There is a hint of summer warmth in the air and, above the cracked and flaky bark on the trunks of the plane trees, fresh green leaves are unfurling. The last of the commuters are hurrying home, but we head a few streets up from Trafalgar Square and along a narrow road of antique and 'oriental' shops named Monmouth Street.

On the left hand side at the far end of the road there is a small shop named Sakura – Japanese for 'cherry blossom'. Surprisingly, the shop is still open. On sale inside are 'exotic' artefacts, a few books, and boxes of incense.

In the back corner of the shop there is a curtain which, when drawn aside, reveals a descending staircase. Down the stairs at the bottom are two small rooms. The one on the right is slightly larger, but still only about four metres square. As your eyes get used to the light, you see that there are about a dozen people crammed into the tiny space. Most are sitting on chairs, but a few perch on cushions on the floor. Midway along the back wall is a lacquered shrine, with candles burning, a vase of flowers, and a small figure of the Buddha.

There is one man in particular who grabs your attention. He is an Englishman in his early forties, but of unusual appearance. He is wearing orange robes over a thick jumper. He has longish, lanky brown hair, and spectacles. But it is his presence that really makes you pay heed. He seems utterly alert, confident, at ease in himself. The look in his eye and the set of his mouth are formidably serious and intent, except that sometimes he catches someone else's eye and breaks into a toothy grin.

After a quick check of his watch, he faces the shrine and in a deep voice chants and bows to the Buddha, the others following his lead. He then sits on a low platform and explains to them about Buddhist meditation. He speaks slowly, choosing and emphasizing his words carefully, but with that same underlying intensity and conviction. The people present are fascinated and, after the few minutes of instruction, shuffle into their meditation postures and close their eyes. He begins the period of meditation by ringing a Japanese bowl. The room falls silent, while above, unseen, the red double-decker buses rumble by and taxi cabs honk their horns.

❧

In the London of the early twenty-first century, Monmouth Street is pedestrianized, full of trendy clothes shops, smart hotels, an internet café, and several beauty parlours. The Buddhist shop and the shrine room are long gone.

But the Buddhist movement that started in that tiny basement has, in the course of 40 years, established well over 100 Buddhist centres and groups in 25 countries,[2] and been at the forefront of bringing Buddhism to the West. This is the story of how it happened.

The man who started it all – and who taught those early classes – was a Londoner born in 1925 and named Dennis Lingwood.

He had an unusual childhood, being diagnosed at the age of eight with a heart condition and confined to bed for two whole years. He spent day after day largely on his own, quietly observing the room around him. To keep him occupied, his parents brought him books. He studied ardently and eagerly, and, once the bedridden period was over, carried on educating himself in the arts, literature, philosophy, and religion.

One day, aged 16, searching through a secondhand bookshop, he found copies of two Buddhist texts – the *Diamond Sutra* and the *Sutra of Hui-Neng*. He took them home and read them intently. As he was later to write – perhaps a little enigmatically – the texts made him realize that 'I was, in fact, a Buddhist and always had been.'[3] It seems they affected him profoundly and opened up a vision that guided the rest of his life.

Europe was now in the ravages of the Second World War, and the young man, despite his supposed heart condition, passed the army medicals and was posted as a member of the signal corps to – of all places – India. Once the war was over, and his unit was due to be disbanded, he left them behind and walked off into the vast unknown of that land – in search of Buddhist teachers. In August 1947, 20 years before the sixties generation would fly out to India in search of spiritual enlightenment, the 22-year-old Dennis Lingwood burnt his identity papers, gave away his few possessions, and 'went forth into homelessness', following the example of the Buddha. With a young Indian friend, he spent two years wandering, mainly in southern India, relying on alms for food and shelter, and periodically settling in one place to study and meditate.

He had a disappointing experience of Buddhist teachers in India; there were not many who seemed interested in teaching the Dharma. But eventually he was ordained as a monk in the Theravada tradition and given the name 'Sangharakshita'.[4] Later, he found his first real teacher – a scholarly Theravadin monk named

Jagdish Kasyap – who was able to guide his Buddhist studies. But then, in the early 1950s, Kasyap left him in Kalimpong, a small trading town in the mountainous borderlands of northeast India, telling him to 'stay there and work for the good of Buddhism'. Sangharakshita did as instructed, and was a keen and able teacher, eventually establishing a vihara,[5] and gaining a reputation for his talks and writings on the Buddha's teaching. In 1957 his first book, *A Survey of Buddhism*, was published.[6] Both then, and in the years since, it has received high praise from Buddhists throughout the world, such as from the scholar Edward Conze who said in a review: 'Without hesitation, without any reservation whatever, I recommend Sangharakshita's book as the best survey of Buddhism we possess at present.' At this time, Sangharakshita also wrote a series of articles that were later published in book form as *The Three Jewels* and *The Eternal Legacy*.[7]

In the late 1950s, many Tibetan teachers were forced into exile as the Chinese invaded their county. It just so happened that they would often come into India via Kalimpong. Sangharakshita had always been interested in all forms of Buddhism and, though ordained as a Theravadin monk, he was now able to meet teachers who practised the Mahayana and Vajrayana traditions,[8] and to receive initiations from eminent Tibetan lamas. Dhardo Rimpoche – who ran a school for Tibetan refugee children – became a particular friend, and Yogi Chen – an eccentric Chinese Chan practitioner with a deep knowledge and experience of meditation – was another influential teacher. Sangharakshita must have seemed an unlikely figure to them: a young Englishman totally dedicated to learning about the Dharma, and to organizing Buddhist activities. But he was happy and at home in this world and could see himself living out the rest of his days there.

However, Sangharakshita's life's work was to be revealed to him in the next decade. He was invited to England to work with the growing number of people interested in Buddhism. There were few Buddhist teachers, especially teachers who understood Western culture and spoke good English. There were hardly any books published on Buddhism, and few Buddhist groups, let alone established centres. Sangharakshita, however, was a Westerner who had been ordained for 14 years. He was ideally qualified to help.

On 12 August 1964 he landed at London Airport (now Heathrow). He had left England during the austerity of the wartime years, and the London he returned to was very different from the city he had known. The skyline was crowded with tower blocks, the streets more congested with cars, the shop windows crammed with consumer goods – TVs, vacuum cleaners, and other domestic electrical appliances.

He soon realized there was growing potential for Buddhism in the UK. What was meant to have been a four-month visit to the Hampstead Buddhist Vihara turned into a year's stay, and then another. Eventually, Sangharakshita decided to remain in the UK and work to establish Buddhism there.

He went back to India for a 'farewell tour', travelling with a close friend named Terry Delamere. But while in India he received a letter from the English Sangha Trust, the organization that owned and ran the Hampstead Vihara and that had originally invited Sangharakshita to the UK. The letter made it clear that they didn't want him back and suggested he stayed in India to avoid any fuss and embarrassment. It seemed there had been gossip about his friendship with Terry, and rumours had spread – never substantiated, and denied by Sangharakshita – that it was a homosexual relationship. There were also tensions around the way Sangharakshita taught Buddhism. Some of the trustees of the English Sangha Trust wanted to establish a strictly 'orthodox' Theravadin monasticism, while Sangharakshita drew on all schools of Buddhism and was much more willing to experiment and to adapt to the different conditions of the West. He'd also made enemies by phasing out the teaching of a particular meditation practice which he believed had caused some people to become 'alienated' – aware of themselves in a forced, mechanical fashion which left them severely out of touch with their emotions, and even, in some cases, leading to mental illness.

Sangharakshita read the letter, turned to Terry and said: 'Do you know what this means? It means a new Buddhist movement.'[9] He'd tried to work within the established Buddhist organizations, but it had been terribly awkward and difficult. Now he could start afresh. He'd been set free. Two of his teachers – Dilgo Khyentse Rimpoche and Dhardo Rimpoche – gave him their blessing.

He arrived back in London in March 1967. Many of those who attended the Hampstead Buddhist Vihara were unhappy with the way he had been treated, and rallied round him. Among them were Emile and Sara Boin, who ran Sakura, the 'oriental' shop in Monmouth Street, in the centre of London. They arranged for one of the basement rooms to be leased, and within two weeks of his return, Sangharakshita was running classes there. On the evening of 6 April 1967, about 24 people gathered and recited a ceremony specially written by Sangharakshita to dedicate the Triratna Meditation Room and Shrine of the Friends of the Western Sangha.[10]

❧

There were plenty of people who had a scholarly or romantic interest in things 'oriental', but Sangharakshita was looking for the ones who wanted to use Buddhism to change their lives. Buddhist organizations up to then in the UK had tended to be 'societies' where you could learn about Buddhism, but that were not necessarily run by committed Buddhists. No doubt such a society might help someone first discover the Dharma and get started on the path, but Sangharakshita wanted to establish a sangha – a community of people dedicated to living out Buddhist ideals, and to taking their practice much further.

Most of those very first followers of Sangharakshita were of an older generation, but it was increasingly the young who were drawn to him, with whom he felt fully able to communicate, and who he thought might be ready for radical change. For these were the Swinging Sixties, a wave of revolutionary change in outlook and attitude that arose first and foremost in the younger generation. They'd grown up in the affluence that followed the austere postwar years, but were not satisfied with the conventional, conformist consumerism that was on offer. The dreams of their parents – a happy family home, domestic comfort, and an annual holiday by the seaside – seemed stifling and dreary to them. They wanted to break out. With their new music, festivals, fashions, and drugs, they created exciting, experimental subcultures of their own.

And so young London was fizzing with a cocktail of ideas: Marxist and anarchist, ecological and psychological, sexual and spiritual. Anti-war protesters chained themselves to the railings of embassies. Psychiatrists took acid trips with their patients. University professors slept with their students. It was exhilarating, idealistic, and open-minded. It was also self-indulgent, naive, and confused.

Sangharakshita was one of the pioneers of Western Buddhism who, along with other teachers such as Shunryu Suzuki and Chogyam Trungpa, was able to communicate with this young counterculture and create one of the first actively practising sanghas in the West. Like many of those first Buddhist teachers in the West, he was unconventional, not to say controversial, willing to experiment and break out of the old Buddhist modes of organization and lifestyle. He was able to meet the young halfway, yet was clear and uncompromising in his communication of the Dharma. That Sangharakshita was sometimes openly critical of the Buddhist 'orthodox' for their over-adherence to old rites and rituals only made him more popular with the young hippies with their 'anti-establishment' sympathies. The time was right for a radical break, for something new and creative to emerge. Sangharakshita was later to say that he 'rode on a crest of a wave' and had he started ten years earlier, or ten years later on, it would have been much harder to have founded the Friends of the Western Buddhist Order.[11]

But in those early days Sangharakshita couldn't have known what form the new Buddhism would take. He gradually learned how to communicate the Dharma to this contemporary audience, and worked out how to make it relevant to them. The new movement had to proceed by trial and error, dealing with issues and problems as they cropped up. All this drew new depths of creativity from him. It was an intense, visionary time of his life which others later described as his 'shamanic period'. In this period he wrote many poems, dreamed vivid dreams, and experienced new levels of inspiration. He grew his hair long and unkempt, with great 'mutton-chop' whiskers; he wore rings on his fingers, tried LSD a couple of times, became sexually involved with some of the young men around him, and went to experimental theatre and film.

Sangharakshita taught several meditation classes every week and gave one or two major series of talks each year. The lectures, which took place in hired halls, drew much bigger crowds than the meditation classes and the atmosphere was often electric. He also led Easter and summer retreats each year at 'Keffolds' – a large country house in the countryside south of London. Over time, with great patience, and also with apparent enjoyment, he would work with the raw energy of the young retreatants, introducing more meditation, periods of silence, and deeper and clearer study of what the Dharma really meant. For many people these were magical, wonderful, life-changing weeks. They were able to experience new levels of awareness and emotional positivity. Bonds of friendship were deepened; people had their first taste of the potential of sangha.

People often arrived on retreat looking tired and tense. By the end of the week, their faces were alive and bright. Then, on the last day, they'd start looking sad again. They didn't want to go back to their old lives! Why couldn't they live like this all the time? So, in 1968 some of the new friends rented a large house in suburban Purley (Croydon) and formed the first FWBO residential community.

People were getting more involved, starting to spend more time together, and friendships were forming. They were having the time of their lives. One week some of them would make a giant, golden papier-mâché Buddha atop a van which they'd take to free festivals in order to advertise the FWBO and its classes. Another weekend they'd be running a jumble sale to raise funds, choosing some of the old clothes to dress themselves up in. Another time they'd all meet in someone's flat, smoke dope, paint themselves different colours, and re-enact the *Tibetan Book of the Dead*.

Gradually, a body of people were building up around Sangharakshita who had at least a little more idea of what a Buddhist life entailed, and who wanted to dedicate themselves to it. The first ordinations into the Western Buddhist Order, the community of committed practitioners at the heart of the FWBO, had taken place in April 1968, and there were more ordinations in August 1969.

It was also a time of tragedy. Sangharakshita's friend Terry Delamere had always suffered from severe depression and had had periods of feeling suicidal. Sangharakshita spent many hours talking to Terry, trying to help him. He had to cope with this alone, as Terry didn't want anyone else to know about his problems. When, on the morning of 14 April 1969, two police officers turned up at Sangharakshita's flat, he immediately knew what it meant. His friend had stepped under an underground train and ended his life. Sangharakshita had lost a dear and close friend; he wept every day for six months and, at the same time, he had to carry on the work with the new Buddhist movement.

In late 1970 the lease on Sakura expired. The FWBO needed to find new premises, but they couldn't find anywhere suitable in time. There followed a period of holding classes in different venues each week. Without a permanent home it was hard to hold the group together, and people started to drift away.

A 15-month period of uncertainty followed, while various people trudged the streets of London searching for a property they could afford. Eventually, Sangharakshita wrote to all the London boroughs asking for help. Two weeks later, in January 1972, a reply from Camden Council requested an urgent meeting. Sangharakshita went with Hugh Evans (later ordained with the Buddhist name Buddhadasa) to view a small, disused factory building in Balmore Street, Highgate. 'Can you do it?' asked Sangharakshita. 'I think so', was Hugh's reply. He gave up his job to become the first full-time worker for the FWBO and to establish the Archway Centre.

Classes continued and Order members started teaching, setting up groups in other British cities, even travelling to other countries. Sangharakshita decided it was time he took a sabbatical. This created a flurry of anxiety among some involved in the fledgling Buddhist movement. Why was their teacher going away? How would they manage to carry on practising without him? He wrote a 'personal message to all friends' in the *FWBO Newsletter*,[12] explaining that he wasn't going because he was worn out, nor because he was disappointed by the slow progress of the movement, but because he wanted to release 'unprogrammed and unprogrammable energy, long accumulating within me'. His diary had been constantly crammed full with classes, appointments, and other scheduled activities. It was time to function in a different way, in order to contact even deeper sources of inspiration. In early 1973 he went with a friend to a chalet in Cornwall.

Sangharakshita remained keenly aware of his other new Dharma-companions, sending them letters and poems, and including them in his meditations. They carried on running the classes back in London, often thinking of him and wondering what he was up to. Then, as summer approached, he wrote and suggested they meet on the solstice.

2

East End Buddhaland

And so this close circle of friends gathered under bright blue skies in the open landscape of the New Forest in Hampshire, eager to hear what Sangharakshita had to say. He too was keen to talk to them about his developing vision for the FWBO, eager to speak in a new way. He was beginning to see the Western Buddhist Order as a tiny manifestation of Avalokitesvara, the Bodhisattva of Compassion.[13] In one of the forms in which Avalokitesvara is depicted in the Indo-Tibetan Buddhist tradition, he has one thousand arms reaching out in all directions, each holding different implements with which to help relieve the suffering of the world. The spiritual community of the FWBO really could be Avalokitesvara made manifest in the world. Each Order member could be like one of those arms, holding his or her own particular implement, working in his or her own particular direction, each part of a greater whole, each joined as one spiritual body. If they were able to work together in this way, the whole would be far greater than the sum of the parts. They could be a tremendous force for good in the world.

～❧

At that time the Archway Centre in Balmore Street was the main centre of the FWBO. They had a temporary lease on the building, in an area due to be redeveloped into a housing estate. Most of the residents had already been moved on. The locality had become a strange ghost town: a mixture of defiant and embittered old residents who wouldn't move out, and students, artists, drug-addicts, and dropouts who'd moved in to squat in the empty houses. There were colourful characters, including Simon who painted half his face red and half blue, and Irish Paul who, despite believing he was an incarnation of the Holy Spirit, broke into the Buddhist centre and stole money. The location had advantages too. Squatting was at that time still legal in the UK and so Buddhist communities started forming around Balmore Street as squats. At one time, there were nine communities associated with the Archway Centre.

However, after a few years, the limitations became more apparent and the Centre sangha began to think of moving on. For one thing, they wanted to be in a safer, less ghettoized area. Stones had been hurled through some of the panes of glass during one meditation session. 'Move away from the windows', said Subhuti, the young chairman of the Centre, who was leading the session. They edged to one side and carried on meditating.

Moreover, they were now thinking of a bigger and more ambitious project. The hunt was on for a new Buddhist centre. Subhuti organized the search for a new property, while another Order member, Lokamitra, undertook the fundraising.

In February 1975, Sangharakshita flew back into the UK from New Zealand where he'd conducted the first ordinations outside the UK. He was met at the airport and driven straight to Bethnal Green in London's East End. There, on the main road, was a huge, many-storeyed, red-brick Victorian civic building – an old fire station that had been empty for five years. Slowly but surely, it was starting to decay. It had become a den where local children and teenagers hung out. The walls and timbers were black and charred where they'd started fires. Graffiti was daubed on the walls. Someone else had painted over the graffiti: 'NO KIDS ON THE ROOF'. It stank of urine. Most of the windows had gone and were boarded over with corrugated iron, which had then been fly-postered.

But to the young Order members showing Sangharakshita the burned-out wreck, this was the new Buddhist centre they were going to build for London. He strongly encouraged them to go ahead. After negotiations, a five-year lease was signed (the first year and then a second being free) and the project got under way.

The plan was to build the largest Buddhist centre in Europe and so create a major focus for Buddhism in the West. Members of the residential community in the top floors would run the public centre below. The centre would have rooms for guests to visit and experience a taste of this full-time Buddhist lifestyle. There would also be a flat for Sangharakshita to stay in, so that he could lead seminars and give talks.

Sangharakshita had emphasized the importance of the arts and beauty in the spiritual life, and so they wanted the centre to be as aesthetically pleasing as possible. The space where the fire engines used to park would become a large and beautiful shrine room, with a Buddha statue sculpted by an Order member named Chintamani. In crafting the statue, he would follow traditional Buddhist forms, and yet also draw on Western artistic and cultural influences.

The *FWBO Newsletter* launched a campaign to raise £30,000, saying:

In the next few weeks a team of eight Order members and Friends will set up camp in the crumbling rooms of the fire station and get to work. Frequent working retreats will be held, and anyone who wishes to help at any time will be welcome to stay. We hope that in this way we will complete the work within a year, or with luck and hard work, sooner.[14]

In the event, it cost more than a quarter of a million pounds and took over three years.

A team of men moved in and started work in June 1975. They slept on the floor on sleeping bags, meditated together in the morning in the skeleton of the old fire station, worked hard all day on its renovation, studied and did puja in the evenings. Sometimes they wouldn't leave the building for days, and they paid themselves only £5 'pocket money' per week. As summer changed from autumn into winter, it got harder; there was no gas – so no heat – and the electricity wasn't connected until Christmas.

The building was in a much worse state than they'd realized. One day Atula, one of the few team members who actually had some building know-how, removed some of the floor timbers. The joists underneath were infested with dry rot.

Intense idealism lived alongside extreme naivety. There was extraordinary determination, and a shocking lack of experience. It was crazy, chaotic, and they often learned the hard way – by making mistakes. There was also tremendous excitement: they were bringing the Dharma to the West, something of great historical importance was happening, and they were right where it was taking place! Sangharakshita named the community *Sukhavati*, 'full of bliss', which is the name of the Buddhaland of Amitabha, the Buddha of the West.[15]

At one stage, the project ran out of money. Although some of the team took on external building jobs to raise more funds, by the end of a year they'd only made enough money to support themselves, and no more work had been done on the building. It felt like they were running just to stand still. Were they going to fail? Was it going to end in humiliation and disaster?

The London Borough of Tower Hamlets came to the rescue with a substantial grant, enabling the employment of a large workforce to complete the project. In addition, the GLC (Greater London Council) agreed to pay for the materials. East End labourers worked side-by-side with 'the Buddhists', bemused that the latter were doing it – happily – for £5 per week.

The building was now taking shape, although the bricks and mortar weren't the most important thing. It was what they'd built between them that was *truly* precious, and it related to what Sangharakshita had spoken of in the New Forest.

They really were building the 'New Society' – a place where more and more people could contact the ideals of Buddhism and live them out. They'd created a 'total situation' together – living, working, practising, and playing as dedicated companions in the Dharma-life. The work had demanded great energy and commitment, and they'd learned how spiritually transformative this could be. Some of them wanted to find ways for that to continue and, as we'll explore later, 'team-based right livelihood' was to become one of the defining emphases of the FWBO. They'd also gained valuable experience in practical matters like building and fundraising, as well as in community living. They'd developed greater confidence in their own potential, and were grateful for the way Sangharakshita had also placed great trust in them, allowed them to get on with it, and make their own mistakes.

The project also generated tremendous inspiration, which radiated throughout the movement. FWBO activities had already gotten started in Brighton, Croydon, Glasgow, Cornwall (southwest England), Helsinki, as well as Auckland and Christchurch in New Zealand. In the mid to late 1970s, centres opened in

Manchester and Norwich, Order members went out to Australia, Sweden, and the USA, and a building team went on from the London Buddhist Centre project to a old farmhouse in the Welsh hills, that was to become Vajraloka, a meditation retreat centre.

Other institutions of the movement were taking shape during this time, such as the 'Mitra system'. 'Mitra' means 'friend', and those who felt a connection with Order members and the FWBO, and who wanted to take their practice of Buddhism further, could, through a simple yet beautiful ceremony, express that aspiration by becoming a Mitra. Over the years, much effort was to be put into providing a three-year study course for Mitras at FWBO centres, and also in encouraging Order members at centres to befriend Mitras to help them to deepen their practice of the Dharma and their connection with the FWBO.

❧

All this time, Sangharakshita was overseeing the young movement. He could now work in a much less 'hands on' way and had more time to write, reflect, and provide teaching and spiritual inspiration. In December 1973, he gathered a group together and led a week-long seminar on the *Bodhicaryavatara*, a classic Mahayana text that emphasizes the altruistic dimension of the spiritual life. Each day they'd sit round in a circle, books in hand, he in robes and carpet slippers, an old reel-to-reel tape machine recording the proceedings, as he guided them carefully through the text, line by line.

Between then and 1990, Sangharakshita conducted 150 seminars either on traditional Buddhist works or commentaries on them, or, occasionally, on non-Buddhist texts. The recordings were later transcribed by volunteers (in itself a huge labour of love) and made available for study. In later years, some of the material from them has been edited into books.[16] The seminar

17

became Sangharakshita's principal medium not just for imparting information about Buddhism, but also for teaching people how to read Buddhist texts, how to reflect on their teachings, and how to think critically. He brilliantly drew out the essentials from a text, revealing its profound depths, while also showing how it pertained to the practical and everyday.

Subhuti was to say of that first seminar:

> … it was the first time I really saw how a Buddhist text could contain a mysterious power, and how well Bhante[17] [Sangharakshita] could release that power for others. If you read the transcript of that seminar now, you might not think it very remarkable, because in the intervening years the ideas have become a familiar part of our discourse. But, in those days, they were dazzlingly new and revolutionary. It was tremendously exciting.[18]

Sangharakshita also carried on giving talks and writing during this time. He has since remarked that it was during this period that he started to feel the FWBO really could make an important contribution to bringing Buddhism to the West, and that his talks therefore became even more inspired and uplifting than in the early days. Sometimes it would take him several hours to come back down to earth after speaking.[19]

There was, for example, a whole series of lectures on the *Sutra of Golden Light*. He wrote a series of articles and book reviews on Western figures such as William Blake in which he started to make connections between Buddhist and Western art and culture. There were talks and booklets in which he commented on social and political issues, such as the 1977 prosecution for blasphemy of the *Gay Times* newspaper. On the tenth anniversary Order convention in 1978, a talk entitled 'A System of Meditation' provided the main model for how the FWBO understands different meditation practices.

People anticipated eagerly the next talk, book, or seminar transcript, and these created waves of inspiration that radiated through the movement. Dharmachakra Tapes was set up in the early 1970s to record all Sangharakshita's talks. In 1973, the movement published its first book – a small collection of talks by Sangharakshita entitled *The Essence of Zen*. From this initial venture grew Windhorse Publications, the FWBO's own publishing house. Spearheaded by Nagabodhi, they published more of Sangharakshita's writings, as well as the *FWBO Newsletter*. Initially producing books using a decrepit old 'Gestetner' copier machine, Windhorse became steadily more professional. At first, their main task was to make Sangharakshita's works available to the new movement, but from the early 1990s to the present day, they have been effective at selling his books and those by other authors they publish in bookstores, actual and virtual, around the world.

In November 1978, the day of the opening ceremony for the London Buddhist Centre finally arrived. Sangharakshita had written a poem especially for the occasion, and gave a talk to an excited audience. There was extensive media coverage, celebrations went on all week, and the meditation and Buddhism classes were packed out from that day on.

3

You've Had the Theory, Now Try the Practice

In 1980, Glasgow FWBO was about to move into its new premises in Sauchiehall Street, right in the city centre. The young chairman, Ajita, presented his report to the AGM.

> No one here, including myself, at least to some extent, realizes just what this is going to do for the Buddhist movement in Glasgow. It is really only beginning to dawn on me as we slowly but surely march on towards completion. Sometimes, in the middle of the night, I wake up with my heart pounding with energy when, just for a moment, like a flash, I see what it will do to the movement and to Glasgow. You know, we've worked really hard over the past seven and a half years and we've done a lot of good

work in the movement and, I hope, on ourselves. But now we are beginning to come out into the open. Now we are beginning to expose ourselves to the great Strathclyde public. I'm completely confident about the sort of effect it will have, not only on ourselves but also on the Glasgow inhabitants. They won't know what hit them.[20]

His report went on to 'foresee on the glimmering horizons of the future' more classes and more people getting involved in the Dharma, more communities, more Buddhist businesses, and more arts activities. The list got increasingly ambitious and visionary as it went on. There would be 'More leisure, joy, and happiness… more creativity and more metta[21]… a renaissance of Glasgow.' And his report ended by asking 'Who else can do it?'

That was what the FWBO was like in those days: a beacon of idealism that attracted more and more people. The fire and passion of Order members like Ajita won over many hearts and minds, and the movement was now growing fast.

~&

In the late 1970s, many Western societies had sunk into economic recession – with mass unemployment and a sense of crisis and decay. The affluent and optimistic hippy era was over. 'Flower power' gave way to punk: hard-edged, angry, and defiant. In the next decade, many countries would elect right-wing governments that advocated free market economics. In the UK, Margaret Thatcher led such a government to power, dominating the political scene for over a decade. Gifted at popularizing her ideas, Mrs Thatcher talked about 'rolling back the nanny state', giving the individual more choice, and freeing the power of the market to create wealth and prosperity. 'There is no such thing as society, only individual men and women, and their families', she was famously quoted as saying.[22] Her government aimed to keep public expenditure low, so taxes could be cut. They reduced the power of the unions, in particular fighting a long and acrimonious battle with the National Union of Miners and the coal-mining communities it represented. The power of local government was curbed, and many public companies and utilities were privatized. Government legislation gave council tenants the right to buy the houses they lived in, and parents the right to have more say in the school their child attended. Arguably, this did create a wealthier society, though one that was also more atomized and individualistic, with a greater gap between rich and poor. The process of change was experienced by many people as a decade of bitter conflict and the defeat of old values. By the end of the 1980s, it had brought about a profound change in social values.

However, the optimism and idealism of the previous era seemed to live on in the FWBO, at least for a while longer. Here, the spirit of the 1980s was dynamic, expansive, and heroic. There were around 150 members of the Order in 1980; by the end of the decade, the number was nearly 400. New centres, communities, and businesses were opening every year. There was a fervent belief in the ability of the Dharma – and especially the FWBO's way of practising it – to change the world. It attracted many disaffected with what was going on in the wider society. The FWBO gave them a context in which to live out their ideals, and a cause to which they could dedicate their lives. They felt intensely grateful.

But, of course, it wasn't all perfect. The UK Buddhist Society had a journal called *The Middle Way*. It had a brownish-yellow cover and contained scholarly articles and book reviews. Turning over the pages in the November 1980 edition, you came across a slogan in big, bold, type: 'YOU'VE HAD THE THEORY. NOW TRY THE PRACTICE'. This less than subtle statement was followed by the contact details of various FWBO centres.[23]

Those few words speak volumes about the state of British Buddhism at the time. The 'establishment' had a predominantly scholarly and intellectual approach to the Dharma and was generally not peopled by those practising Buddhism. However, there were other more practice-orientated Buddhist groups emerging, of which the FWBO was by far the largest. Believing that they were the ones who were *really* doing Buddhism and showing the way, their youthful enthusiasm sometimes bubbled over into cockiness. Someone in the UK Buddhist scene even dubbed them 'the storm troops of British Buddhism'. It probably wasn't intended to be a compliment, but the revolutionary young Buddhists of the FWBO were rather pleased with the label.

Sangharakshita's encounters with other Buddhist groups had never been entirely happy. He'd met many good and impressive individual Buddhists in India, but he was mainly disappointed by organized Buddhism which seemed stuck in a lazy formalism. He'd experienced the same on his return to England. There had been difficulty within the FWBO too. In its early days it had invited in a number of teachers from different traditions. During one retreat, a Japanese Zen teacher had suddenly announced that he was the Buddha Maitreya with new truths to impart, and this caused considerable confusion.

So Sangharakshita was not only critical of much of the rest of the Buddhist scene, but also protective of his fledgling movement. As one of his disciples was later to write:

> Sangharakshita's characteristic tone [was] more embattled – at the time of his seminal writing and the foundation of the FWBO he was isolated and much criticized. He was an intense visionary figure who felt that, virtually alone, he must transmute Asian Buddhism into the language and archetypes of the West …[24]

Sangharakshita would never condone unfriendliness or unkindness, but he did encourage people to speak out and be critical if necessary. 'Honest collision is better than dishonest collusion' was one of his aphorisms of the time.[25] Criticism of the ideas and practices of another faith, or of a different Buddhist tradition or teacher, didn't necessarily imply intolerance or lack of respect.

No doubt there were all sorts of confused ideas about Buddhism in the milieu of the time. The Dharma was coming into a new culture and there were bound to be misunderstandings and, consequently, a great deal of clarifying and explaining to do. The FWBO was active and outgoing, and Order members took part in inter-Buddhist activities and conferences, wanting to get to know and befriend other figures in the UK Buddhist scene. But sometimes the young FWBO's tone of discourse slipped from strong-minded into strident. 'The FWBO appears to have a reputation for being somewhat abrasive in its contacts with Buddhist groups', wrote one Order member. 'This is not a reputation of which we are particularly ashamed since we have found, over the years, that all that goes by the name of "Buddhist" is not necessarily so. We have regarded "common platforms" with circumspection and have felt it essential to voice our criticisms of what we consider to be muddled, woolly, or just wrong.'[26]

Another issue was the frictions that inevitably occurred when people lived so closely and worked so hard together. These led to clashes, interpersonal difficulties, and disagreements. And since they believed that being Buddhist entailed working to change oneself, any difficulties required honest communication and exploration, rather than avoidance. The young Buddhists were intense about the intensity. Despite their best intentions, very painful disharmonies could occur.

Sangharakshita's response to this during the 1980s was to emphasize spiritual friendship as a vital part of the path to Enlightenment. He gave a talk on the theme, and led two seminars on relevant texts from non-Buddhist sources, one on 'The Duties of Brotherhood in Islam' and the other on Samuel Johnson's 'Ode to Friendship'. In 1984, he also gave a seminal paper on Buddhist ethics, published as *The Ten Pillars of Buddhism*.

But the hardest lesson the young FWBO had to learn was in Croydon, a suburb of south London. There had been a community there from the very earliest days, but in the mid-1970s, Order members such as Nagabodhi and Vessantara went there to run more public classes which rapidly took off. In 1978, Padmaraja became the chairman of the centre. He was capable and charismatic, and activities continued to grow under his direction. In 1981, they moved into large new premises on Croydon High Street. In the same complex, they ran a wholefood shop and Hockneys, a vegetarian restaurant which gained a reputation as one of the finest in the country. The businesses made money, which allowed for further growth. In 1984, Independent Arts was founded. It became a highly successful arts centre, drawing well-known artistic figures of the day to give talks and performances, and attracting crowds from all over London to suburban Croydon. The following year, the Croydon Centre expanded again, and purchased Rivendell, a retreat centre in rural Sussex.

For the 30 to 40 people who worked there, especially in the restaurant, it was a pressure-cooker situation and the heat was up high. They worked long hours, coming home late to communities where often they lived three or four to a room. The next day they were up early to meditate and off to work again. This was not a temporary state of affairs while they established a new project, but how life went on year after year.

The end began to justify the means. All the hard work required in running so many activities took over, and people's spiritual well-being and integrity were often sacrificed. The show had to go on, and so management structures grew more rigid, communication more harsh, the culture more stultifying.

A complex and unhealthy group dynamic developed, as described by Vishvapani who worked in the restaurant:

> Before starting work at Hockneys, I had felt an outsider, now I discovered there were spheres within spheres. An inner circle clustered around Padmaraja, and then there was a pecking order, in which the more senior parties ensured the conformity of the junior. This was enforced through teasing, sarcasm and undignified nicknames ("Roy the boy", "Baz", "Plonker" – it really was like school) as well as appeals to loyalty and idealism. We were, after all, "building the New Society" – what undertaking could be more worthy? The sometimes vicious bullying was masked for perpetrators and victims alike by the idea that criticism or "fierce friendship" was a form of spiritual practice.[27]

One's 'loyalty' to the Croydon Centre was constantly questioned and challenged. One person, when they asked to become a Mitra,[28] was met with 'You say you want to be a Mitra, but I do not see the person who will commit themselves.'[29] If you decided to leave, you could be told you were a coward, not big enough to deal with the demands of intensive spiritual practice.

Through the 1980s, Order members elsewhere in the FWBO were becoming increasingly concerned with what was happening in Croydon. The difficulty was that all FWBO centres had been set up as legally and financially autonomous. This had been done to encourage the taking of local responsibility and avoid over-centralization. But it meant that there was no one who could just march in and demand change. Moreover, Padmaraja commanded such loyalty and devotion that it was feared he might be provoked into making the Croydon Centre independent of the FWBO.

Then there would be even less that could be done to influence the situation.

In 1988 Manjunatha became the men's Mitra convenor for Croydon. This entailed him attending FWBO-wide meetings where he encountered criticism of the Centre. Once back home, he started to voice his own reservations. Gradually, the group mentality started to unravel. Sangharakshita asked Manjunatha to encourage Mitras who had been bullied in various ways to write to him personally, so that he'd have firm grounds for challenging Padmaraja. More people began to speak out.

Then, quite quickly, Padmaraja resigned from the Order and there were some others who left too. A few of those had been badly traumatized by their experience. The majority stayed involved with the FWBO and worked painfully through feelings of shame, failure, or betrayal.

There was one important institutional change that took place in order to prevent such a thing happening in the future. In the early 1990s, senior and experienced Order members were appointed by Sangharakshita to be 'Presidents' of the main FWBO centres. They would mainly act as 'spiritual friends' to those centres, giving advice, encouragement, talks, and teaching. But they would also retain an independent view of the situation, and so act as a safeguard against things going wrong again.

There might easily have been a tendency to scapegoat Padmaraja, but, on the whole, this was avoided. As *Golden Drum* (the magazine that had now replaced the *FWBO Newsletter*) reported at the time: 'The hows, whys, whens, and whos of the matter will provide fuel for much serious reflection over the coming months, not just in Croydon, but throughout the movement in Britain.'[30] Indeed, at Order gatherings there was lengthy and repeated discussion, shock and soul-searching. What had gone wrong? How had it happened? They analysed the personalities involved, and puzzled over the intricate group dynamics; how had they let themselves be taken in? It was a major loss of innocence for the FWBO.

Some of those who'd worked at Croydon had felt a level of camaraderie and common purpose that they would rarely experience again; yet there had also been bullying and intimidation. How strange and sad it was for them that something so good and well-intentioned could go so badly wrong. They had to learn how idealism needed to be tempered by experience. They had to understand more fully the complexity of group dynamics, and the mixed nature of human motives. These were painful lessons to learn.

4

The Indian Dhamma Revolution

A group of Westerners are driving with their local guides in a jeep through the heart of India. Their vehicle shakes and slithers for hours down bumpy, ridged roads. The landscape is mainly flat, with large fields of sugar cane and cotton. There are banana trees with ragged leaves blowing in the breeze, and mango trees with their smoky fronds of flowers. A large green lizard stomps into the undergrowth. Every few miles, the jeep passes through another village, with its assortment of mud-brick buildings and market stalls.

These dust-red roads are the veins along which the lifeblood of India beats. There are women marching forwards with babies strapped to their backs. Emaciated, absent-minded cattle saunter across the road. Men teeter on bicycles overladen with sacks of rice. There are bullock carts with great lengths of sugar cane strapped across them. A cranky old bus, crammed with passengers, races to pick up those waiting at the next stop. Not everyone can fit on, and some are left behind, breathing the red dust and blue exhaust. Women with palm branches sweep, in a dignified manner, the debris from the front of their tiny settlements. An old man with silver stubble on his chin hobbles along; one of his feet is badly swollen, and throbbing painfully. The jeep passes a truck piled high with bananas, enough to fill a whole house. There are beautifully poised girls with pots and pans perched on their heads, and spirited young boys running excitedly to keep up with the jeep. And, all the time, the sun beats down onto the hot dust.

Eventually the jeep turns off the main road onto a smaller, bumpier track that seems no more than a succession of potholes. It arrives at another village where it comes to a stop and everyone clambers out, stretching tired and cramped limbs, but smiling at the group of locals who are there to meet them. The Indians look curiously at them, while the Westerners look wonderingly at their surroundings.

In the middle of the settlement there is a clearing towards which the group is now heading. There is a makeshift stage at one end, decorated with yellow and orange fabrics, fairy lights, and pictures. Some are pictures of the Buddha, but there are also images of a modern-looking Indian, with a round face, thick-rimmed spectacles, and wearing a suit.

Gradually, as evening falls, more people gather in the square. It seems like the whole village is there, and there is noise, chatter, and excitement. Some of the Indian men get up onto the stage and there are speeches of welcome and introduction. Then a few of the Westerners also climb – a little shyly – onto the platform and, one by one, they speak.

It turns out that they are Buddhists too. They tell their audience that the Western countries from which they come are not Buddhist. They are very rich countries where people have all they need materially. But often people are still not happy; they feel something is missing. And that is why they have chosen to be Buddhists – to give spiritual direction and purpose to their lives.

They have also learned that while Buddhism had died out in India hundreds of years ago, in the 1950s a man called Dr Ambedkar led a huge number of his poor and downtrodden people away from the oppression of the caste system into the freedom of Buddhism. They have been very moved by this story. It meant a lot to them to hear that Buddhism could have such a strong social message, and so powerfully affect large numbers of people. And so they have come to see that movement for themselves, and to meet some of those new Indian Buddhists.

There is laughter and applause as each of them finishes speaking. The two groups – Western and Indian – look at each other with smiles on their faces. You can't tell who is the most amazed: the Westerners at being given such a warm welcome by total strangers in the middle of this vast land, or the Indians at meeting Westerners who are so interested in them, and who share the spiritual path they have chosen.

❧

How the FWBO, founded as a new Buddhist movement for the West, became established among some of the poorest people of India is perhaps the most unexpected chapter in its history. To explain how people so socially, culturally, and economically far apart can end up practising in the same spiritual community will require giving some background in recent Indian history, making this a rather long chapter. However, it is an extraordinary story you are about to read. More people are now in touch with the movement in India than anywhere else in the world. If the content and structure of this book was to reflect the numbers of people involved, this would be a book about the movement in

India, with perhaps a chapter or two on the FWBO in the West, rather than having been written the other way round.

❧

The point at which we'll begin our account is in London in the mid to late 1970s – the era of the building of the new London Buddhist Centre, and the heady days of establishing the new FWBO. In 1976 Sangharakshita gave a series of talks about the *Sutra of Golden Light* under the heading of 'Transforming Self and World'. He used the images and stories of the sutra to show how you needed to change yourself in order to have a beneficial affect on the world, but that you also changed yourself by being active in the world. The work of transforming self and transforming world went together.

Sitting in the audience, and listening intently, was Lokamitra. To him, the talks were groundbreaking; they opened up a pathway through the apparent conflict between self and other.

Ordained in 1974, he had worked as a school teacher, but left his job in order to work for the FWBO. As a friend of his described him at the time, 'Lokamitra was a bull and a whirl-wind of a man, combining an incendiary disposition with a total dedication to the cause he had espoused.'[31] But then he became ill and his doctor told him he needed an operation. He took up yoga as part of a regime to improve his health and avoid the need for medical intervention. After a year, he'd not only cured himself, he'd become an accomplished yoga practitioner and qualified teacher into the bargain.

In 1977, he travelled to India with some other FWBO yoga practitioners to attend a course led by the famous yogi BKS Iyengar. He asked Sangharakshita if there were any of his old Indian friends and acquaintances he'd like him to look up while they were there, and Sangharakshita made some suggestions. On

14 October they were on a train that stopped in Nagpur. There seemed to be a big Buddhist celebration going on there, and they wondered what it was all about.

They knew very little about Dr Ambedkar and the movement he led, in which hundreds of thousands of 'Untouchables' converted to Buddhism. But they were about to learn much more about him, to experience his movement first hand. They were also going to discover a whole new dimension to the life and work of their own teacher, Sangharakshita.

The origins of the caste system are unclear, but for a thousand years at least it has been a defining feature of Hinduism and therefore of Indian society. It comprises four *varnas* ('colours'): Brahmanas (priests, known in English as Brahmins), Kshatriyas (warriors), Vaishyas (traders), and Shudras (the menials and workers who are in the vast majority). Outside the system are those considered non-caste Hindus (the 'Untouchables'), as well as other tribal people, and those of other religions. Within this main structure are all sorts of subdivisions and tribal loyalties; it is estimated that there are between two and twenty thousand different castes.[32]

Underlying the system is a supposed hierarchy of religious purity. The Brahmins are closest to God and, being most pure, have a duty to perform the sacred rituals. At the bottom are those least pure of all; for caste Hindus to come into contact with them would be polluting, debasing their own level of purity. Hence there developed the idea of 'untouchability', and the extreme disdain and hostility that was directed towards these people. They dwelt in slums on the edge of villages and had to do the most dirty and menial work. They lived in fear of the harshest punishment if they transgressed their place in society. Marriage took place only within caste, which perpetuated the whole system. It meant that for 'Untouchables' (and for Shudras too), there was no hope of bettering oneself, or escaping their hellish situation. As an 'Untouchable' you were, quite literally, treated like dirt.

At the end of the nineteenth century, partly as a result of the British colonization of India, there were a few cracks in the system. For example, up to 1893, the British army recruited 'Untouchables' into the army. It was into this world that Bhimrao Ambedkar was born on 14 April 1891.[33] His father, Ramji, married to Bhimabai, had risen to the rank of subedar-major in charge of a military school. They were Mahars, one of the largest 'untouchable' castes from the Maharashtra region of central India.

Bhimrao was the fourteenth and youngest child of the family (seven had died in infancy). He was much loved and grew up bright, intensely competitive, and determined.

After 1893, army policy on 'Untouchables' was reversed and the family had to leave the school and move away, though the army did find Bhimrao's father a job as a storekeeper. His father's position also enabled Bhimrao to be sent to school and given access to an education. This meant that he had a much less severe experience of caste discrimination than those in the villages, though he did tell some shocking stories from his school days: how he had to sit just outside the classroom away from the other children, or how – when being given a drink – he'd be instructed to hold his head back and mouth open, so that water could be poured in without the bottle having to touch his lips. At Government High School, he had no friends and the teachers ignored him. He buried himself in his books and studied intensely.

In 1905 a marriage was arranged with Ramabai – he was fourteen, she was nine. Their son was born in 1912 and named Yashowant. He was the first of five children, though the only one to survive into adulthood.

Aged 17, the young Ambedkar was the first 'Untouchable' to matriculate from Government High School, Bombay (now

Mumbai). He caught the attention of liberal-minded reformers and obtained a scholarship to study at the University of Bombay, gaining a BA in English and Persian. He won further scholarships to attend Columbia University in New York City (where he studied economics and social science), Grays Inn in London (to train as a barrister), and the London School of Economics (where he was awarded an MSc and then a doctorate in economics). He also learned German and spent a short while studying at Bonn University.

These would be extraordinary educational achievements for someone from even the most advantaged background; for someone who was born 'untouchable' it was unbelievable. Life in America and Europe was enlightening in other ways too. For the first time he was free of caste; he could mix freely and socialize with other students, allowing him to notice the much more equal roles of men and women. It was also a hard time: his life in 1920s London was austere and he worked long, lonely hours with fierce determination.

Ambedkar arrived back in India hoping to launch a career and financially support his family. He was to be bitterly disappointed. Earlier, between studying for degrees abroad, he had taken an administrative job for the Baroda State and had come up against caste discrimination. He had terrible trouble finding anyone who would rent him rooms to live in. Clerks in the office behaved offensively towards him, sometimes throwing books and papers across the room onto his desk, rather than having to come into closer contact with him. Finally, the situation escalated and he was threatened with physical violence. He was forced to leave. Later, he tried to set up a law practice, but it took months to get a single case.

Terribly disillusioned, he saw how all-pervasive caste was, how strong the hatred and fear it engendered in people. As highly educated as he was, it made no difference to how he was treated.

The prejudice and discrimination he'd suffered would have broken many. It upset him greatly, but made him only more determined to work politically for the uplift of his people.

The India of that time was in social and political ferment, especially with the campaign for independence from the British gaining momentum, alongside growing communist and left-wing movements. Ambedkar had always followed these debates, but now he threw himself in fully. He was a nationalist; he wanted a free India – but an India that would be free for *all* its peoples. Independence had to be accompanied by democratic and legal structures that ensured this. He often clashed with independence leaders, most famously with Gandhi, who argued that Hindus would reform the caste system. Ambedkar was deeply sceptical of this and argued that the 'Untouchables' needed to free themselves. He formed alliances with the communists and others campaigning for the uplift of oppressed peoples, though as time went on, he became more critical of how they interpreted all issues solely in terms of class, not understanding the especially pernicious effect of caste – with its religious sanction and psychological debilitation.

He led or took a prominent part in high-profile actions, such as the 1927 'Chowder Tank Case' in which a group of 'Untouchables' drank water from a tank reserved for caste Hindus. Another protest involved the public burning of the *Manusmrti* – the Hindu text that contains laws and injunctions regarding caste, some of which are horrific, such as pouring molten lead into the ear of an 'Untouchable' who has overhead the sacred texts. In the course of his life, Ambedkar was closely involved in the formation and election campaigning of three political parties.

In 1935 Dr Ambedkar's wife died. She was only 40 years old. His family life was turbulent and tragic; of his immediate family, only he and Yashowant were left, and his son was afflicted with rheumatism. Ambedkar felt great regret that he wasn't able to do more for his family.

By this time the British were realizing their days in India were numbered, and they were working out how to withdraw and grant independence. Recognizing Ambedkar's stature as a leader of the 'untouchable' community, and also his legal and political abilities, they invited him to participate in a round-table conference along with Gandhi. This led to further clashes about how those outside the caste system would be represented in a new India. In 1942 Ambedkar agreed to join the British wartime administration in India. Many reviled him for collaborating with the British, but he saw the defeat of Nazism as the immediate priority. He was made Labour Minister, initiated many progressive changes, and was seen to be an extremely competent administrator and legislator.

So it was that, when Nehru became the first Prime Minister of independent India in 1947, Ambedkar was invited to be Law Minister. He was, quite simply, the most able and qualified person for the job. For the next two years he chaired the committee that framed India's new constitution, and, with widely admired skill and dexterity, saw it through the legislative process. He didn't get everything he wanted, but he was a pragmatist and did what he could. The result was a democratic constitution for the new India that has given stability to one of the largest, and most diverse and complex, countries in the world.

During this time, Ambedkar's health was beginning to deteriorate. At a clinic he attended, he met Dr Sharda Kabir, who became his second wife in 1948 and who cared for him in the years ahead.

Next he started work on the Hindu Code Bill, which he hoped would reform marriage law, the rights of women to divorce, own property and open bank accounts, and other social practices which he believed enshrined inequality in Hindu society. But it provoked fierce opposition from the more conservative and extreme Hindus; they would allow an 'Untouchable' to frame their new constitution, but not to introduce social legislation.

Nehru prevaricated and gradually withdrew his support; at the same time, Ambedkar was becoming increasingly disillusioned with the government's policy towards Pakistan and Kashmir, and its growing relationship with Russia. In 1951, when it became clear that the legislation was going to fail, Ambedkar resigned in disgust. The government was trying to 'build a palace on a dung heap',[34] he famously said in his resignation speech: they were bringing in legislation that would be ineffectual because they didn't dare to change the underlying social laws.

In his early life, education and personal uplift had ended in disillusionment; now Ambedkar saw the limits of political change. Caste was an attitude of superiority and arrogance on the one hand, and of fear and worthlessness on the other. Caste was inside people's minds, and no amount of law-changing could force people's minds to change. What was needed was a form of transformation that went much deeper.

His resignation from the cabinet marked the end of his life in politics, but the most radical and significant step in his life was yet to be taken. Not that this step was unprepared. As early as 1927, there had been debate within the 'untouchable' movement about whether a religious conversion away from Hinduism would be necessary, and Ambedkar had joined the debate. In 1935 he made his famous statement: 'I was born a Hindu and have suffered the consequences of untouchability. I will not die a Hindu.'[35]

Throughout this time he was studying the major world religions, considering which one would give his people a fresh start and a positive spiritual ideal. There was speculation about which way he would go, and even offers of financial help for his people from leaders of some faiths. In the late 1940s, he began to write and talk about Buddhism more frequently, and it became clear that that was the direction in which he was being drawn. Buddhism was not based on superstitious beliefs, argued Ambedkar, but on the morality that was needed to underpin genuine freedom, equality, and solidarity between peoples. It was also rooted in Indian culture, so conversion would not be socially divisive or destructive of the best of Indian heritage.

In 1954 he finally announced his intention to convert to Buddhism, and two years later, on 14 October 1956, he took the refuges and precepts from U Chandramani, the most senior monk in India at that time, and then led 480,000 followers in those same refuges and precepts and 22 additional vows. Another 200,000 converted at Candrapur the next day, and Ambedkar predicted massive waves of conversion. Fresh hope was in the air. In the words of someone who was there:

> I cannot describe what I felt that day – I do not have the words in English – but it was as if our lives started anew. After so many centuries, people who had been treated as slaves and outcastes came to know that we are no less than anyone else. That was a great change, and what we gained was confidence in ourselves.[36]

Ambedkar's health was failing: he suffered from diabetes, rheumatism, high blood pressure, heart problems, and severe leg pain. Yet still he pushed onwards, working late into the night, studying and writing. Only six weeks after the conversion, on the morning of 6 December 1956, he was found collapsed at his desk. Ambedkar was dead, and his new Buddhist movement was without a leader.

Among the new Buddhist community there was no one else of Ambedkar's stature, no one with his understanding of the Dharma and its potential. The rest of the Buddhist world did not understand the new movement and did very little to respond, offer encouragement, or give teaching.

Ambedkar's people were utterly shocked and traumatized by his sudden death. But somehow the memory of what he had done for them lived on, and they wanted to honour that memory. The movement continued – through political action, social and educational projects, and more Buddhist conversions. Today, millions of people revere Ambedkar as a 'modern saviour' and travel on pilgrimage to the Dikshabhumi ('place of conversion') in Nagpur. Inevitably, there were different interpretations of what Ambedkar had intended and tensions between the more 'political' and more 'spiritual' approaches, so that today Ambedkarism is alive and kicking, if also complex and fragmented.

'Untouchability' was made illegal in the new constitution fostered by Ambedkar, and it also made other provisions for these people, such as a guaranteed quota of places in higher education and jobs in government service. Today, attitudes have begun to change, especially in the fast-growing modern cities. But old habits die hard and many Dalit[37] communities have not yet shrugged off hundreds of years of stigma and found confidence. The old caste discrimination lives on, especially in the villages of India.

❧

In the 1950s Sangharakshita was living in a north Indian hill town named Kalimpong, but travelling south at times to give talks or for other engagements. He had corresponded with Ambedkar during the 1950s and met him on three occasions. He remembers Ambedkar as sharp, fierce, and by necessity grimly determined, though greatly loved and trusted by the people around him. They talked about Buddhism and especially about what conversion entailed, and how the ceremony should be organized. Ambedkar asked him to conduct the initial conversion ceremony, but Sangharakshita recommended he ask U Chandramani, the Burmese monk who had conducted his own sramanera[38] ordination and who was the longest ordained – and therefore most senior – monk in India.

By chance, Sangharakshita was in Nagpur on the day Ambedkar died. On hearing the news, 100,000 people gathered at a meeting that had been quickly arranged. Sangharakshita was invited to speak. Other speakers were approaching the microphone, but were so upset and demoralized they could hardly speak. Many just burst into tears. The atmosphere was one of utter dejection. Then it was Sangharakshita's turn. He realized that it had fallen to him to try and lift their spirits, to remind them that Ambedkar's life need not be wasted, but that his life's work would live on in them.[39]

He addressed many more meetings in the next few weeks, and for the rest of his time in India (from 1957 to 1964), he spent up to six months a year in Maharashtra teaching the Dharma to Ambedkarite Buddhists, forging a connection with them that they were not to forget. Their faith in the Dharma inspired him deeply. He later wrote to a friend:

> My own spiritual experience during this period was most peculiar. I felt that I was not a person but an impersonal force. At one stage I was working quite literally without any thought, just as one is in samadhi [deep meditation]. Also, I felt hardly any tiredness – certainly not at all what one would have expected from such a tremendous strain. When I left Nagpur I felt quite fresh and rested.[40]

Eventually, he was invited to go and help establish Buddhism in the UK. He could see the potential there, and there were limitations as to what was possible in India. The Ambedkarite movement had become increasingly politicized, the Republican Party of India that Ambedkar had founded had split, and Ambedkar's prominence in India and beyond was now fading. Sangharakshita decided to return to the West, yet hoped he would be able to return one day and continue the Dharma work in India.

❧

Over a decade later, in October 1977, Lokamitra and his friends were on their journey to India to study yoga. By sheer coincidence, they turned up in Nagpur, in the very place of Ambedkar's conversion to Buddhism, on the very day of the twenty-first anniversary of that conversion. Later that day Lokamitra was taken to a huge gathering of half a million people, was urged up onto the stage, said a few words of greeting, and talked about the movement Sangharakshita had started in the UK. He was amazed by people's response to Sangharakshita; they remembered him from his India days and obviously felt a high regard for him.

The day after that rally in Nagpur, Lokamitra revisited the scene and wandered around, thinking through what he had witnessed. It had affected him profoundly. Here were thousands of people who were eager to practise the Dharma, and for whom it could make a great difference to their quality of life. He had found a situation of huge potential for 'transformation of self and world'. As he later put it: 'I did not consciously decide to live and work in India then, but I have no doubt that my future was decided that day.'[41]

While attending the yoga course in Pune, Lokamitra met more of Sangharakshita's old friends, started giving Dharma classes and talks, and even set up and led a retreat. When he returned to the UK he asked Sangharakshita if he should go to India and start a centre in Pune, and received strong encouragement. So, in August 1978, along with two other Order members – Padmavajra and Kularatna – he returned to India. There was great excitement and anticipation, as reported by Kularatna:

> We were given a rousing send-off from the London Buddhist Centre. The atmosphere was festive, and everyone seemed aware of the significance of the occasion: that the Dhamma[42] was travelling from the West to the East. We were showered with streamers and escorted out of Bethnal Green by a honking motorcade of rather decrepit but colourfully decorated vehicles, to the bemusement of the local population – some of whom joined in with a wave.[43]

Arriving in India, Lokamitra was slightly more accustomed to the place than the other two, who were in culture shock, trying to learn to live with the heat and humidity, the din and disorder, the sights and smells, the shocking poverty, and the sheer numbers of people – a great mass of humanity being born, living, and dying on the streets right in front of their eyes. But they launched straight into action, taking up to 14 classes per week, Lokamitra leading the way, while the other two learned as they went along. The first classes were held in tiny shacks or garages of corrugated iron, packed out by whole families, including children and grandparents. They were shown great hospitality, and met with an enthusiasm and religious devotion that they were quite unused to in the West.

The next year they invited Sangharakshita to visit, and so he returned to India after an absence of 12 years. He officially inaugurated the movement there which, instead of being called the FWBO, was to be known as Trailokya Bauddha Mahasangha Sahayaka Gana (TBMSG) – the 'Association of Helpers of the Spiritual Community of the Three Worlds'.[44] He conducted the first ordinations into this Order[45] on Indian soil, and travelled around giving many talks. His Western disciples gained a new insight into their teacher. They were astonished at the thousands of people who turned up to welcome him and hear him speak, and amazed by how much at ease he seemed with India and its people:

> The atmosphere at his lectures was a highly charged mixture of enthusiasm and devotion. Thousands of people attended and would offer him countless marigold and jasmine garlands. Whenever he made a particularly impressive point ... the crowds would burst into spontaneous applause and laugh delightedly. Though simple, his lectures were never simplistic ... In whatever he said one could feel that his sole purpose was to communicate the means by which people could transform their lives.[46]

It was the first of a number of visits that took place through the 1980s and 1990s.

It was obvious to Lokamitra from early on that it wasn't enough just to teach the Dhamma; they had to also create conditions for a decent human life among the people. A number of Order members arrived from the west to see if they could help: Virabhadra (a doctor), Padmasuri (a nurse), and Vajraketu (who helped set up organizational and administrative structures) began working in the slums of Dapodi, providing basic health care and advice about nutrition. The social wing of TBMSG – known as Bahujan Hitay ('for the welfare of the many') – was under way.

The movement started to grow. It is perhaps hard for Westerners to understand the courage required of the first generation of Indian Order members who gave up their 'conventional' jobs to come and work for the movement. In a culture without the social security provisions many are used to in the West, giving up a secure job in order to work for a new and unknown Dalit organization was a big risk.

They also had to contend with prejudice, corruption, and caste discrimination. For example, retreat facilities that they had booked would suddenly be double booked once the officials realized they were Ambedkarite Buddhists. Sometimes they were just up against endless bureaucracy. In 1980 a Buddhist family in Dapodi offered Lokamitra land for building a vihara. It took three years and countless arguments with officialdom to get the property transferred to TBMSG. The authorities insisted that all 35 owners of the land had to gather in one place in order to complete the transfer. Then the government decided to reserve the land for a fire station and bazaar, which meant more legal arguments.

It wasn't until eight years later that building work was able to begin. But finally, in 1990, the Mahavihara opened in Dapodi. To have their own purpose-built place was a big step forward for the TBMSG. One of the first big programmes that ran there was a one-year training programme for people who'd asked for ordination, and who wanted to work full-time for the movement. This created new teams of trained and committed workers who were able to greatly expand both the social and Dhamma-teaching work. New generations of Order members, who came from the communities in which they were working, were taking increasing responsibility for running the movement.

Earlier, in 1983, they had also managed to establish a retreat centre – the Saddhamma Pradeep Retreat Centre. Located in a deep forested valley below the famous Buddhist caves of Bhaja, it was able to house up to 150 people. In 1992 the Hsuan Tsang Retreat Centre opened at Bor Dharan, near Nagpur, able to cater for up to 350 people. Another major facility is the Nagarjuna Training Institute at Nagpur.

Costs at these retreat centres are kept low to enable anyone to attend. It is perhaps hard for a Westerner to imagine how revolutionary a retreat may be for an Indian. Many people will undertake a long and arduous journey to get there. For many women, it may even be the first time they have been away from home. For a woman to travel away from home by herself can arouse suspicion, even hostility, among male relatives; this is one reason why the retreats are single-sex.

❧

All this work of building facilities for Buddhist practice and conducting social work required money, and there was precious little of that among the new Buddhists in India. In 1985 Loka-mitra travelled to Taiwan and met an old friend of Sangharakshita's. Dr Yo was extremely helpful, and set up dozens of meetings with Taiwanese Buddhists who were very happy to give money to the Indian Buddhist movement. This area of fundraising has spread to Malaysia, Korea, Japan, Thailand, the USA, and even the Tibetan community in India. A number of Indian Order members, as well as Lokamitra, travel to these various countries each year as emissaries.

The other major source of fundraising was a charity – Aid for India – which, at Lokamitra's request, was founded in the UK just a year or two after he'd gone out to India. In 1987, the charity became Karuna Trust,[47] the name by which it is still known today. Karuna is one of the big success stories of the FWBO. According to the Buddhist commentator Stephen Batchelor (writing in 1994), 'In terms of the sheer numbers of people affected, the most extensive social action project undertaken by Buddhists in Europe is that of the Karuna Trust.'[48]

Karuna has focused on one particular method of fundraising – the door-knocking appeal. A team of four to eight men or women volunteers gather in a house in a UK city. For the next six weeks, they live, eat, meditate, study Dharma, train, and socialize together – looking after each other as they prepare for the evening's work when they go, on their own, to their allotted streets to knock on doors and ask people if they'd like to give money to Karuna. They leave a brochure with those who might be interested and go back a day or so later to see if they want to ask more questions, or commit themselves to making a regular donation.

The appeals have become something of an institution in the UK FWBO, with a twofold benefit. First, each appeal raises tens of thousands of pounds for welfare projects in India. Secondly, the appeals can be life-changers for those who take part in them. Knocking on a stranger's door in a strange city and asking for money can seem a terrifying prospect, but the appeals are skilfully designed to give participants the training and support – all within a context of Buddhist practice – in how to communicate confidently and from the heart.[49]

In 1981, the first appeals made about £35,000. By the mid to late 1980s, they were raising over a quarter of a million pounds each year.[50] Today, the charity's income is nearer £1.5 million.[51] In the 1990s, Karuna started to receive grants from UK charity trusts and government development agencies, although donations from individuals and door-knocking appeals still account for 70% of their income. While it is still the major funder of TBMSG projects in India, the charity has also broadened out its remit. It now funds other Dalit-led projects, as well as working with other similarly marginalized communities in countries such as Bangladesh, Nepal, and Tibet.

This financial relationship between a UK charity and an inexperienced Indian Buddhist organization hasn't always been easy. On the one hand, Karuna has obligations to its donors. Equally, under charity law, it must clearly account for the money it spends. On the other hand, the Indian movement is still financially dependent on the West; especially in the early days, its people were unused to running projects with big budgets. There is plenty of room here for tension and misunderstanding, and the territory has had to be negotiated through much sensitivity and discussion.

❧

It is not possible to do justice in this one chapter to the work in India: the health and education facilities; the women's projects;

the legendary Dhamma teaching tours round towns and villages, which in turn have sown the seeds of Dhamma centres; the retreat facilities; the attempts to break out of TBMSG boundaries and make links with other scheduled castes; and the establishment of training processes for men and women to go for refuge and be ordained into the Order. India is where the FWBO/TBMSG is in touch with the largest numbers of people, and where it has the greatest potential to affect the lives of many more.

There have also been, and will continue to be, many challenges for the wider Ambedkarite Buddhist movement, and for TBMSG as one of the communities that make up that wider movement.[52] First, there is what could be called the 'challenge of legitimacy'. Some have questioned if what Ambedkar taught was truly Buddhism, or merely his socialistically inclined ideas with a spiritual dressing. Usually his main emphasis was on the need for strong ethics and morality in order to foster values such as respect and solidarity necessary for a truly democratic and just society. He gave very little emphasis to, for example, meditation, ritual, or the concept of karma.

However, Ambedkar was communicating Buddhism to an audience with very particular needs and circumstances. To tell some of the poorest and most oppressed people in the world that their suffering was a result of craving would be nothing less than insulting. For generations, Hinduism had taught these people that they'd been reborn as 'Untouchables' due to sins in a past life. Even though Buddhist ideas about karma and rebirth might be very different, it would be hard to convey this, and an emphasis on those teachings might only have put them off Buddhism.

Ambedkar, who'd spent years studying the Pali texts and other Buddhist works, had to translate the Dhamma for his people and the situation they found themselves in. What they needed first of all was a vision of life that gave them the self-respect and confidence to build a more free and just society. Ambedkar knew that the political and social revolution required a spiritual revolution: 'Ambedkar himself was a deeply religious man; he believed that religion was essential to human life.'[53]

But within Ambedkarite circles the debate is focused not so much around whether Ambedkar was true to the Dhamma, but around the correct interpretation of his ideas and, in particular, the balance between political and spiritual activity. The Ambedkarite scene can be highly factionalized, with politicians using the movement to further their own agendas and interests. TBMSG has had to function within a complex and potentially explosive political scene. At times it has been accused of an overemphasis on the spiritual, diluting Ambedkar's political work and distracting people away from it. There has also been suspicion of its connections with, and origins in, a Western Buddhist movement.

Defenders of TBMSG will point to Ambedkar's insistence on the need for a spiritual dimension, and to the social and psychological uplift it has given to people. They could also point to similarities between the thinking of Ambedkar and Sangharakshita. Both have reinterpreted Buddhism for new times, drawing on Buddhism as a whole, rather than one particular Buddhist tradition, in order to achieve this. In this task, both have striven to get to what is essential to the Dhamma, stripping away the cultural accretions. Both have stressed the vital importance to the world of spreading the Dhamma, and have been critical of the apathy and ineffectualness of much of established Buddhism. Both founded Buddhist movements which encouraged full engagement with the Dhamma regardless of lifestyle; lay Buddhists were not just to be nominally Buddhist.[54] Sangharakshita has also written of Ambedkar's influence on his own thinking, helping him to see more clearly the social and political dimensions of the Dhamma.

Secondly, there is the 'challenge of caste conditioning'. Will the conversion movement go deep enough, or will centuries-old caste attitudes continue within the new Buddhist communities?

For example, the Matang, Chambhar, and Mahar scheduled caste communities in Pune have all become Buddhist, but they have remained largely separate from each other, with few common Dhamma activities, or intermarriage. TBMSG has had to do much work in this area, holding seminars and events to unravel and unknot the psychology of caste. There will need to be a constant effort to overcome the weight of conditioning and to encourage people to keep reaching out beyond their own communities.

Thirdly, there is the 'challenge of secular assimilation'. This is the danger that when the new Buddhists achieve social and economic security and join the fast-growing Indian middle-class, they then settle down into that, forgetting both the Dhamma and the need to help those less fortunate than themselves.

So far, TBMSG seems characterized by great energy, determination, and generosity. But perhaps – just as in the West – accommodation with the comfortable and materialistic surrounding culture will be a danger. There needs to be a continual emphasis on the radical, altruistic dimension of the Dhamma.

A final challenge is that of differences in conditioning between those Western Order members active in India, and the Indian Order members themselves. For example, many of the Westerners have had an education and upbringing that gives them a natural capacity to set up and run organizations. Many of the Indians have very different conditioning, and have much less natural organizational ability, though in contemporary India this is changing quickly. However, this disparity can cause tensions around leadership, initiative, and how decisions are made.

Despite these challenges, so much has been achieved in just 50 years of this new Buddhist movement and around 30 years of TBMSG Dhamma work. Before the great conversion there were less than 200,000 Buddhists in India[55]; now there are estimated to be up to 20 million.[56] The new Buddhists seem to have done well educationally and economically compared to non-Buddhist Dalit communities. Buddhist ideals and practice have helped them to lift themselves up. All this is especially impressive given the lack of education, resources, and access to Buddhist teaching that they started with.

Within this wider Ambedkarite movement, TBMSG is increasingly well-known and respected. Through its Dhamma work it is in contact with hundreds of thousands of people, and its social work is widely admired. That a fledgling Western Buddhist movement continued the work of a great Indian political, social, and religious leader seems an incredible, unlikely story. It has given Sangharakshita great pleasure and satisfaction. As he expressed it:

> I used to ask people, months or even years afterwards, 'What difference has becoming a Buddhist meant for you?' And nine times out of ten they would reply, 'Now that I am a Buddhist I feel free.'

That seems to be the most important aspect of the experience: a sense of freedom. They felt socially, psychologically, and spiritually free.[57]

5

Getting the Dharma to Work

In the early 1970s a television crew filmed Sangharakshita walking through the City of London, accompanied by the interviewer who asked him about the arrival of Buddhism in the West. As they passed the Bank of England and the Stock Exchange, Sangharakshita pointed across at them, saying, 'This is what we're up against.'

If the Dharma was going to be truly and fully established in the West, a movement was needed that enabled all aspects of life – personal, social, cultural, political, and economic – to be transformed. Sangharakshita spoke of the FWBO as building the 'New Society', in which could be found the ideas, practices, and institutions that really enabled people to lead a different kind of life. The first part of this chapter tells the story of the FWBO's attempts at 'transforming work'. It then goes on to discuss other aspects of 'lifestyle' and how people in the FWBO have explored a variety of ways of living a truly Buddhist life in the contemporary world.

Many of the young Order members of the 1970s had university degrees and had just started careers in education, social work, or the arts. But as the FWBO grew, many of them left their jobs to start working for the movement. A number of cooperative businesses were founded in order to create an economic base and to show how Buddhist values could permeate all areas of life and society. The names of the businesses had the hippy flavour of the times: Rainbow Decorating and Rainbow Transport in Croydon, Rainbow Restaurant in Norwich, Sunrise Restaurant in Brighton, Friends Foods in London, and Friends Gardening in Glasgow.

Wanting to live a simple life and to raise funds for Buddhist activities, they paid themselves very little money. A typical arrangement would be to live in a community where meals would be provided and basic needs met, to have a certain number of weeks per year on retreat, and £5 'pocket money' per week. Often the businesses depended on one or two key people who had relevant experience or acumen, and once they moved on, the businesses foundered. The failure rate was inevitably high, and yet the number of projects slowly increased.

By the end of the 1970s, living in a community and working at a centre or in a cooperative business was the norm; it became how an Order member functioned in the world. In 1980 a three-day 'business seminar' at Padmaloka brought together cooperative workers to discuss the expansion of the FWBO's economic activities. They calculated that to support 1,000 people, they'd need businesses with a combined turnover of at least £4.5 million. And they assumed that was exactly where the movement was heading:

> Obviously, at the rate at which we are currently expanding, we are soon going to want to be supporting at least that many people within our 'New Society', not to speak of undertaking and capitalizing new projects both in the UK and abroad.[58]

Since the FWBO had little capital, the kind of ventures that got under way tended to be low-investment, labour-intensive businesses, which also meant low profit. In 1980 a new business was founded in London with the aim of generating larger amounts of money to fund the fast-expanding movement. Windhorse Trading started as a market stall. Known these days as Windhorse:Evolution, its turnover is in the region of £10 million, and it has been by far the biggest and most successful experiment in right livelihood in the FWBO.[59]

The market stalls – in Camden Lock and Covent Garden – sold imported gifts. Soon the business expanded, selling wholesale at trade shows and from a van that travelled the UK visiting gift shops. The import nature of the business meant goods had to be paid for three months in advance of them arriving in the warehouse, regardless of whether they were actually sold on. Cash flow was a perennial worry. For many years the Windhorse bank account was to be in the red, with the exception of a few months around Christmas. Arranging and managing the bank overdrafts and business loans was a perpetual strain.

In 1985 the business moved to Cambridge, and Vajraketu and Ruchiraketu arrived to support Kulananda, who was then managing director. Vajraketu involved himself in business operations, while Ruchiraketu's role was to provide spiritual support for the workforce, particularly by exploring how they could make the work into a spiritual practice and a means of personal growth and development. For a small business in a precarious state of existence to employ a member of staff to look after people's spiritual needs was a bold investment.

At a trade show in February 1986 they made what was, for them, a big breakthrough. A buyer from WH Smith – one of the largest UK book and stationery retail chains – approached their stall and ordered 40,000 desk organizers. It was an order worth £30,000 – the biggest they'd ever taken. They were over the moon, until they realized that they didn't have enough money to buy in the stock. Nor would the banks lend it to them.

But a few stalls down at some of the trade shows at which they'd been exhibiting, a businessman had noticed them. Allan Hilder was intrigued and attracted. What were these young Buddhists doing trying to set up in business? He liked their 'give it a go' attitude, and a friendship developed.

So, when Vajraketu was desperately trying to finance the purchase of stock for WH Smith, it was Allan who lent the money. The deal was on again, and Windhorse made what was – for them – an enormous £13,000 profit.

In 1987 Kulananda left Windhorse to become chair of the new Buddhist centre in Cambridge, leaving Vajraketu as managing director. The following year Vajraketu noticed an empty shop in Cambridge city centre and, knowing that Windhorse was overstocked at that particular time, approached the landlords, explained he was from a charity and asked if they would take a very cheap rent. The offer was accepted and the first Windhorse shop – known as 'Evolution' – was opened with huge success.

So, almost by accident, the Evolution phenomenon began. Over the next ten years and more, many UK centres were to form teams to run 'Christmas shops', which traded under the name 'Evolution'. In the early 1990s Britain was still in the process of emerging from a long recession, so it was possible to get cheap, short-term leases. A team of Buddhists could then try out working together, and some money would hopefully be made – the profit being split 50–50 between Windhorse and the local FWBO centre. Very often, after running a Christmas shop, a team would want to stick together and a more permanent lease would be negotiated. By the end of the 1990s Windhorse had a chain of 17

Evolution shops, mostly in the UK, but also in Dublin (Ireland), Essen (Germany), and Valencia (Spain).

The wholesale side of the business – via trade shows and van sales – was still much larger, and that was growing exponentially too. In 1992 the business appeared in a register of the top 100 fastest growing UK companies, with sales rising 37% on the previous year. By 1997, after five more years of rapid growth, Windhorse employed over 190 Buddhists and turnover grew by another 31% to £9.9 million.

❧

A day in the life of an Evolution shop worker would start with a team meeting and arranging the rota for the day's work: perhaps a delivery to unload, boxes to check off and unpack, a new range of goods to be displayed in the shop, cashing-up and banking, and serving customers. In a way, these were ordinary tasks, being carried out in hundreds of other shops down the same street and in the local shopping malls.

There were differences as well. The morning meeting would also include a reporting-in session where team members could let the others know how they were, perhaps sharing something of what was going on in their inner and outer lives. Once a week they'd have a longer 'right livelihood'[60] meeting, and sometimes a staff member from Windhorse headquarters in Cambridge would visit to see how the team was doing and to offer help and encouragement. In these meetings there would be more time to talk about the spiritual aspect of the work: how to use the tasks you were engaged with as a means to develop clearer communication, to use one's time and energy with more awareness, or to respond to one another with greater kindness and cooperation. Teamwork was a strong aspect of the ethos – sharing both the vision for the shop and the work involved in fulfilling that vision, and seeing how you could be much more effective when working in harmony and cooperation. Through all this, people got to know each other better, and strong friendships would often develop.

In the busy period around Christmas a sense of excitement could build up. In the staffroom at the back, a chart displayed week-on-week comparisons with last year's sales figures. Could the team do even better than last year? A lot depended on how well they worked together. More sales would bring in more profit, which they all knew would go to fund Buddhist projects, including their own local FWBO centre. When it flowed, it was fun: at the sales desk they'd be serving a growing line of customers holding African carved wooden animals, bathroom mirrors decorated with pieces of mosaic, scented candles, wind chimes made in Bali, or Indian embroidered cushion covers. Out back was a team of volunteers from the local Buddhist centre who were furiously ripping open large boxes, and unwrapping and pricing-up the contents, so that they could continuously restock the shelves.

✢

For many people in the FWBO during the 1990s, Windhorse: Evolution provided training in how to bring spiritual practice into everyday life, a shared project in which friendships were forged within a relatively simple, focused lifestyle. Sangharakshita, wanting to support the venture, conducted a special seminar for Windhorse:Evolution staff in 1994, exploring the topic of work as spiritual practice. He was later to speak of 'team-based right livelihood' as one of the distinctive emphases of the FWBO.[61] He was obviously pleased to see people able to live their lives so wholly in a Buddhist context and also, in a small way, exemplify to the wider world a different model of economic and working life.

People from all over the FWBO world – from Australia, India, or Mexico – came to work at Windhorse:Evolution to experience a 'full-time Buddhist life', and also to be nearer the ordination training retreat centres (discussed in Chapter 6). The business became an important locus for the meeting of cultures, helping to ensure the spiritual unity of the FWBO. At times, there were people from twenty or more different countries working together at their base in Cambridge, and they generated millions of pounds profit that financed the purchase of many new Buddhist centres, such as those in Birmingham, Manchester, Nottingham, and Sheffield.

Success brings its own tensions and difficulties. By the late 1990s, there was a growing sense at Windhorse:Evolution that they were overstretched and in danger of becoming business-driven, not people-driven. They'd grown so fast that systems and structures had not been able to adapt quickly enough, the management was overcentralized and sometimes, by their own admission, not able to respond with enough care and sensitivity to the needs and aspirations of those who worked for them.

A decision was made to enter a period of 'consolidation'. It is difficult for a business to stand still, but Windhorse:Evolution decided not to try for more growth until they had the necessary conditions to support people to achieve it. One major undertaking they did have to complete, however, was the move of their offices and warehouse to new premises, as the lease was ending on the old ones. In June 2002 they held the dedication ceremony for 'Uddi-yana' – large, brand-new, purpose-built premises on an industrial estate in Cambridge, with a rent bill of nearly £1 million per year.

Other changes were going on within the FWBO as well. While these were seen most clearly at Windhorse:Evolution, they were taking place elsewhere too. A seismic shift in the culture of the FWBO was underway. What used to be the normal 'FWBO life-style' – living in a community and working in a team-based right livelihood – was now becoming a minority activity. Not only had the FWBO broadened out and attracted increasing numbers of people with families and conventional jobs, but many of those who had been living this 'FWBO lifestyle' seemed less willing to do so.

The surrounding society was now more affluent and more concerned about pensions and long-term financial security. Many in the FWBO were less willing to work for a low level of financial support; they were getting older and worried about their future. Some had worked in relatively low-skilled work for a number of years and wanted to develop new skills and make fuller use of their talents. Sometimes an FWBO business had been founded by someone with a strong vision for the spiritual potential of teamwork, but once this person left, the vision faded. The work became rather ordinary and dull, and people wondered what was so special about it. Not all the teams had functioned so harmoniously and some people wanted to get away from painful and stifling team dynamics.

As people moved away, those left behind struggled to recruit replacements and to manage the increased workload. Often they had to start recruiting non-Buddhists onto the staff, when what had attracted those remaining to the business was the enjoyment of working together with other Buddhists. This led to a further loss of morale and more departures.

By 2003, four Evolution shops had closed, four others had non-Buddhist teams, and in most of the others, only a minority of Buddhists were left working. For those who were left in the shops and at Cambridge, these were difficult times that brought into question much of what they'd been working so hard for. There were real worries that the business might not survive at all. Ratnaghosa, the well-respected former Chair of the London Buddhist Centre, was asked to go to Windhorse:Evolution to help Vajraketu and other members of the management team.

Gradually, a creative and pragmatic response to the changing situation emerged. There were many dimensions to this: in management and team structures, opportunities for training and career development, and increased emphasis on fair trade. But one of the major changes was in the systems of financial support.

Until then employees had been 'on support', which meant getting your rent, utility, and food bills (usually while living in a community) paid, being funded to go on six weeks' retreat and holiday per year, and receiving about £30 'pocket money' per week. The underlying principles were of living a simple life and practising generosity. 'Give what you can, take what you need' was the maxim; if you did need more, you should make a request and there would be discussion and dialogue.

This might have worked fine for a small band of friends pioneering a new project to which they felt a strong personal connection. But it was much harder to maintain in an organization that employed more than 200 people and had been going for more than 20 years. For example, one person might ask for four months' extra leave in order to help run an ordination retreat; their manager grants the request because they trust it has arisen out of an altruistic motive. But next week another person approaches the manager because they've just heard that their friend got extra leave. Can they have it too? But the manager believes they are much less engaged in the business and suspects that they just want an easy life. To make fair decisions on these kinds of issues required hours of dialogue, or resorting to an increasingly complex set of rules and regulations.

The language of 'support' and 'pocket money' had evolved way back in the 1970s when most people working that way were young and single, with no dependants. For those who were older, or for those who had partners or children, something different was needed. The system of 'having basic needs met' and making requests for extra expenditure began to make some people – on both the management and the workforce sides of the relationship – feel they were 'infantilizing' people and not letting them take responsibility for basic life decisions. It could also feel difficult to make a request for extra support when you knew everyone in the business was working so hard to make money to give to worthy causes. Sometimes, the dynamic of the system seemed to favour 'give what you can' over 'take what you need'.

Changes were made. First, Windhorse:Evolution has turned the necessity of employing non-Buddhists into a positive opportunity to provide meaningful, ethical work in a friendly environment. (A few of these non-Buddhists have become interested in Buddhist practice; in 2009, one man who became a Buddhist through working at an Evolution shop was ordained into the Western Buddhist Order.) The non-Buddhists who work at Windhorse:Evolution often value the emphasis on fair trade and the education and social projects that the company now funds in some of the developing countries in which it trades.

Everyone who joins the business – Buddhist or not – does so on the basis that they are in agreement with the new 'ethos statement' which outlines five principles that Windhorse:Evolution is trying to embody. The first principle is generosity; everyone is there because they support the vision to make money for good causes. They also want the business to be an expression of Buddhist ethics – the second principle. Thirdly, they see the work as a means to personal development; everyone there is encouraged to use the situation to actualize their human potential. The fourth principle is collectivity and communality; the way the business works is as a series of interlinked teams with a common vision. Finally, there is a principle of commercial viability; none of this will be possible if it is not sound and well-run as a business.

Within this common overall framework there is a choice of how to relate to the business. Some will be happy and able to lead a simple life on support, though there is now a more self-governing system of allowances for 'extras'. Others may prefer to work for hourly wages, which are set at a level comparable to a similar job in a conventional company. A few people in managerial positions are on salaries. There is a pension policy for all employees and the opportunity of longer retreats for those who have been working in the business for a number of years. It is all designed to make Windhorse an attractive place to work, and especially to make it viable as a long-term option.

Currently, of about 220 people employed full-time in the Cambridge headquarters and in Evolution shops, around 150 are Buddhist and 70 non-Buddhist.[62] More than half of the Buddhists are still on support, and nearly half still live in communities, although there are also large numbers – especially in the shops – who are on wages or a salary.

It has been a brave attempt to reapply the principles of 'give what you can, take what you need' to a new time and situation. It is still the case that the managing director 'earns' less than many of the warehouse staff. Even those who are on wages or salaries could probably earn more elsewhere, but are happy to work at Windhorse:Evolution because they value the ethos and its effect on the working atmosphere.

By around 2006 Windhorse:Evolution had revived, with a full workforce, full communities, and morale high again. They started planning to take the business into another phase of growth – in particular, a big expansion in the Evolution shop chain. Yet another huge challenge arose: in 2008 many Western economies suddenly went into recession. In the UK, companies like Windhorse that import goods from overseas were particularly hard-hit by the fall of the pound, as well the drop in sales in main shopping streets. The company had to retrench and quickly revise its plans for expansion. While internally Windhorse has never been stronger, the external business environment has never been tougher. The business could go under, or it could emerge from recession well-placed to grow and thrive once more.

༄

Other recent innovations in right livelihood have been based around mindfulness-based therapies – teaching mindfulness meditation techniques to help those suffering from depression, addiction, chronic pain, or stress. These new developments have especially taken off at the London Buddhist Centre's new Breathing Space and with Breathworks, based in Manchester.

To tell the story of Breathworks, we'll need to go back to the mid-1980s. Prue Burch was a bright and confident New Zealander in her twenties just starting out on a career in the film industry. There was one complication: as a teenager she'd sustained a spinal injury and since then had suffered ongoing pain. Now her back condition had further deteriorated and she was lying in a hospital ward, feeling lost and alone.

> I was in an intensive care ward, surrounded by critically ill people who were moaning and fighting death. It was like a hell realm. I had never been in this sort of situation before, so there was also the shock and bewilderment of unfamiliarity. In the midst of all this suffering, there I was, sitting up in bed, wide awake, wondering how I could possibly survive the next few hours, and willing myself just to cope.
>
> I spent some hours on what felt like the edge of madness debating with myself whether I could get through the night – one voice saying, 'I can't do this. It is impossible. I can't last until morning. I'll go mad.' Another voice was saying, 'you have to,' over and over again, for what felt an age. It was one of the most intense and demanding experiences of my life.

Then, suddenly, out of that chaos and tightness there irrupted a sense of lucidity that contained the message, again as a voice: 'You don't have to get through till morning, you only have to get through the present moment.' Simultaneously my experience completely changed. It was like a house of cards collapsing, and all that was left was space. Suddenly the moment had changed from an agonized, desperate, contracted state to one that was soft, full, relaxed and rich – despite the physical pain.[63]

She knew she wanted to learn to meditate. The hospital chaplain taught her a visualization exercise, which further changed her life, helping her to realize she could work with her state of mind. This path of discovery eventually led her to the Auckland Buddhist Centre of the FWBO, and from there to a five-year period living at Taraloka Retreat Centre in the UK. She was also ordained, receiving the name Vidyamala, and ended up living in Manchester, making films about Buddhism and the FWBO.

However, in 1997 there were more complications with her back and she ended up in hospital again. With this came another spiritual crisis, an echo of what had happened 20 years before. Vidyamala saw that her meditation had become terribly wilful. Her underlying belief was that if she just made enough effort, she would attain higher states of consciousness and avoid pain. 'I was straining to escape my experience and I manipulated the teaching I received to collude with that,' she says.[64] It was spiritually humiliating to realize that this wasn't going to work.

Part of her difficulty was that she'd not met anyone in the FWBO with the experience to understand her needs, and thus able to give her appropriate advice in meditation. But around this time she discovered the work of Jon Kabat-Zinn, a scientist who was bringing mindfulness meditation into healthcare in the USA:

> There was something in his approach about turning towards your experience that I needed to hear at that point ... Now I realize it was all there in our teaching, but I hadn't heard it, or chosen to hear it, or it hadn't been brought out fully enough ...

She felt as though she had to learn to meditate all over again, being more open to her experience, even when that included pain. If you brought mindfulness and kindness to bear on that experience, you could distinguish between the 'primary suffering' of physical pain, and the 'secondary suffering' that was your anguished reaction to the pain – anger, despair, fear, or anxiety. Even if you couldn't make the primary suffering go away, a more creative response to the secondary suffering could transform your life.

Vidyamala also realized that she now had something to offer other people in the FWBO and beyond. In 2001, with a grant from the Millennium Commission, she founded Peace of Mind, running courses at the Manchester Buddhist Centre that used mindfulness and metta meditations to help those suffering from chronic pain. It was immediately apparent that many students found this approach extremely helpful.

Sona, the President of the Centre, was impressed and inspired by the work Vidyamala was doing. He also sensed its huge potential. At this time in the FWBO, team-based right livelihood was in steep decline. Perhaps Vidyamala's work could be developed into a new way for Buddhists to work together. As well as running Peace of Mind courses, perhaps they could also train others to run the courses, eventually creating a community of trainers. In this way, they'd be able to help many more people suffering from pain, and they'd also create for themselves and the other trainers a livelihood which made a direct connection between their working life and their spiritual life: they'd be using their own meditation skills and experience to help others. Interest in mindfulness-based therapies was growing rapidly in the medical and psychological world, with an expanding body of research showing evidence of their efficacy. The time was exactly right for such an enterprise.

Joined by Ratnaguna, they formed Breathworks in 2003 and began running training events at UK retreat centres.[65] Right from the start, these were oversubscribed. They asked those training what they wanted and were surprised – and pleased – to hear that people wanted rigorous, high standards of training, with supervision, course work, and a requirement to complete a number of retreats before they received accreditation.

Only five years later, Breathworks has about 50 fully qualified trainers, with another 140 in training. Most of these are FWBO Buddhists, but some are Buddhists of other traditions, and some are non-Buddhist healthcare professionals. Many of the qualified trainers are now working to deliver 'Living Well' programmes for those suffering from chronic pain. There are also 'Living Well with Stress' courses being provided for staff of the Norfolk Mental Health Trust and at Cardiff University. Since 2006, Breathworks trainers in Dublin have been running a 'Living Well with Multiple Sclerosis' course with funding from the MS Society. The project is also being taken to a number of other countries, such as Germany, India, New Zealand, and Sweden. Vidyamala has published a book in the UK, and already has publishing deals in another five countries.[66] Breathworks is legally constituted as a 'Community Interest Company', which means that any profits are used to serve the community of people who suffer from pain and stress, not the company owners.

Vidyamala is clear that what Breathworks offers is not an alternative spiritual path to the FWBO, though for some people who attend a 'Living Well' course, it may be a doorway into Buddhism. But for many people, the courses can be life-changing – giving them tools with which to better cope with pain and illness. It is also providing a meaningful livelihood for a growing number of people. They have been surprised by the extent to which the trainers experience themselves as a team working together, and they want to maintain this sense of community, seeing themselves as a new team-based right livelihood in the FWBO.

❧

'Lifestyle' has been debated widely in the FWBO. Ironically, for a movement with 'commitment primary, lifestyle secondary' as one of its founding principles,[67] there has been a history of tension around the lifestyles people have chosen to lead.

The majority of people involved in the early days were young and single; this often made those who were older, or who had families, feel that the FWBO didn't really welcome them. It was one thing to create a radically simple, committed, shared Buddhist lifestyle and to promote its advantages. But, in the early days of the FWBO, this sometimes tipped over into a zealous advocacy of community life, and a dismissive attitude toward those who wanted to live differently.

So much idealism and hard work went into building the 'New Society'. In the early days, many centres and projects had a precarious existence – one or two people leaving them could jeopardize their very survival. This put pressure on anyone who wanted to leave in order to have a family, or get a conventional job; and it was hard for those left behind to view leavers' actions impartially.

There had been awareness of the gradual shift in lifestyle patterns, and of the tensions that existed, for quite some time. In 1994 Sangharakshita had given a talk on 'Fifteen Points for Buddhist Parents' in recognition that more people were now having children and so practising in a family context.[68] He also recommended to his close disciples a book by Reginald Ray, an American Buddhist practitioner and scholar.[69] He drew their attention to the book's analysis of the structure of the traditional sangha; here was a model by which to understand the unity and diversity of the contemporary FWBO community.

Ray argues that the traditional sangha comprised 'forest renunciates', 'monastics', and 'lay people'. Each made their particular contribution to the overall well-being of the sangha, and each helped to counteract the spiritual dangers inherent in the other lifestyles. The forest renunciates were totally dedicated to meditation, keeping the ideal of pure and uncompromising spiritual practice alive for all. The danger was that they could become isolated and focused solely on their individual spiritual progress. The monastics cared for the texts, and taught the laity – thus ensuring their support for Buddhism and the recruitment of the next generation of monastics and forest renunciates. But if they weren't careful, they could end up bogged down in institutional matters, losing touch with both spiritual ideals and worldly reality. The lay people could help to keep the monastics and forest renunciates aware of changes and developments in the wider society, and also provide the economic support for the continuance of Buddhism. However, they needed to take care that they didn't succumb to the pressures and distractions of worldly life.

What comes across in Ray's account is that this dynamic between the three different 'lifestyles' could be strained. Even in the Buddha's time, there was friction between the monastics and the forest dwellers about who was *really* leading the spiritual life, and dispute between the monastics and the lay followers over which teachings the latter were given.

Leading members of the FWBO, such as Subhuti, sought to apply this to the FWBO context. [70] There were a few people living a life mostly on retreat. There were quite a number who lived in communities and worked in Buddhist projects – not quite monastic, but maybe 'semi-monastic'. And there were those who lived with partners or families, or who had conventional jobs. As in the Buddha's time, there was likely to be tension. But the aim was to value each lifestyle and be able to see what it brought to the sangha, and also to be honest and realistic about the dangers that came with it. The sangha needed to be aware of how those leading different lifestyles could challenge and counteract each other in spiritually useful ways.

❧

The reality of bringing the Dharma to work didn't turn out anything like the dream of those young Order members at the late 1970s 'business seminar' who imagined the enterprises they'd need to create in order to support 1,000 people in the 'New Society'. According to a recent survey,[71] while 80% of the early generation of Order members in the West had some experience of working in team-based right livelihoods, 55% of the most recent generation (i.e. those ordained within two years of the 2007 survey) have never had any such experience.

People's living situations have followed the same patterns: 97% of the older generation had experience of living in FWBO communities, compared to only 50% of the newer generation. Of those who took part in the survey, 30% currently live in communities, 20% live on their own, and 50% with a partner or family.

There are signs of other new 'lifestyle' developments. There is a steady increase in those living a more 'forest renunciate' lifestyle, at least for a period of their lives. A number of Order members have now undertaken long retreats of a year or more. Naganaga is a women's community in New South Wales, Australia, where women lead a more retreat-like life, and make their facilities available to others who want to do a longer retreat. Situated on a ridge sloping down to the Macleay River, the land around the community is wild and beautiful: kookaburras fly through the eucalyptus trees, big lizards bask in the sun, duck-billed platypuses live in the river. Lokuttaradhatu is a women's community in New Zealand that overlooks snow-capped mountains. Describing themselves as a 'community of hermits', those who live there combine practice and retreat by themselves with more communal activities, and also run practice days for people from the local FWBO sangha. Again, there are facilities for people to go and live there to do longer retreats. Guhyaloka is a men's community in Spain where there is a similar combination of individual and communal practice time, and, each autumn, a three-month retreat for male Order members which is becoming an increasingly valued part of the life of the Order. There is also an annual one-month retreat for female Order members at Akashavana, the women's ordination retreat centre (discussed in Chapter 6).

As we've seen, while there are some new developments in team-based right livelihood, a majority of members of the Order now work outside the FWBO. They combine Buddhist practice with the demands of their job, and often make an impressive contribution to the world through the work they do. In the Order are fundraisers for major charities, filmmakers and writers, teachers and nurses, management consultants, psychiatrists and counsellors. Sometimes they have been able to offer their expertise and perspective to those working in the FWBO.

The result is a richer mix from which everyone can learn. Most people in the FWBO value this new breadth and diversity, and hope that each 'lifestyle' will remain strong and able to contribute to the overall culture of the FWBO.

6
Trouble with Angels

In the 'counterculture' of the 1960s and 1970s out of which the FWBO arose, everything that seemed 'normal' and conventional was turned upside down as people sought freedom in political, psychological, sexual, and artistic spheres. Traditional ideas were thrown up in the air, and nowhere more significantly than with the changing roles of men and women and the emergence of feminism. Forty years later, it is easy to take the current status quo for granted and to forget how hugely men's and women's roles in society have changed in the past few decades.

Women had agitated for political equality – the right to vote – in earlier decades, but in the late 1960s, the women's movement re-emerged. They campaigned for equal pay, employment rights, and other legislative changes. They also argued that 'the personal is political' and challenged the roles that men and women ascribed to each other. The 1960s and 1970s were also a time of sexual experimentation, contraception becoming more widely available, the beginnings of gay and lesbian liberation, ideas of 'free love', and questioning of the dynamics of the nuclear family.

In coming to the West, Buddhism had to adapt to a culture that was not only very different to the more traditional societies of Asia, but was itself in flux. One of the main differences it encountered was in attitudes to sex and gender. This chapter explores how the FWBO sought to make that adaptation, and tells the story of the FWBO's development of separate 'wings' for men and women.

❧

Most people involved in the FWBO in the 1970s were in their 20s and early 30s. Not only were they young, with hormones abounding, they were living in an era of sexual liberation, of 'going with the flow' and 'letting it all hang out'. This wasn't always conducive to 'stillness, simplicity, and contentment' (the positive phrasing of one of the Buddhist precepts).

For the first few years of the FWBO, all the activities were organized for men and women together. Then, in the mid-1970s, one of the squatted communities around the Archway Centre ended up – more or less by chance – being men only. Almost to their surprise, the young men discovered that they enjoyed it. It reduced anxiety around the whole area of sex, needing to impress women, and compete with other men. They started to feel free of their tendency towards emotional dependence on women. It enabled an easier camaraderie among them, which made deeper trust and communication possible. Other men's communities formed, and then women's communities. Experimentation with 'the single-sex idea' was beginning.

The men seemed to develop single-sex activities and facilities more quickly than the women – at least initially. This created some tension between them at the Archway Centre. Some people didn't like the men 'pulling away' and the prospect of segregation. The single-sex idea was hotly debated.

The building of the new London Buddhist Centre, and the communities and work teams that formed through that project, brought men together even more closely. Then, in June 1976, a large house in the sleepy village of Surlingham, Norfolk was purchased. It became Padmaloka Retreat Centre. Sangharakshita held some seminars for women there, but it was a men's community that lived at Padmaloka, and was mainly, and then solely, a place for men. Later, the facilities for training for ordination developed much more quickly for men than for women. There were training retreats at Padmaloka, and four-month long ordination retreats in Tuscany from 1981, and then at Guhyaloka in the Sierra Altana mountain range in southern Spain from 1986 onwards. Even by the late 1970s, and certainly by the early 1990s, a strong and vigorous men's wing of the Order had emerged.

The women's wing did, as we'll see, develop similar facilities, but it took longer. In the early days, it seemed that classes in Buddhism and meditation drew in larger numbers of men than women (whereas the opposite is true in many centres today). Perhaps the men were more easily attracted to Sangharakshita, and he could relate more easily to them (though many women say he was always encouraging of them too). But it was certainly the case that, initially, more men than women got involved. This meant that the men's facilities developed faster, which attracted more men ... and a self-perpetuating situation evolved. Sometimes, women lost their confidence by making unhelpful comparisons with the success of the men.

❧

Back in the late 1970s, the original plan for the London Buddhist Centre project was to have both men's and women's communities in the top floors above the public centre. But then, as the fundraising and building were just about to start, a decision was made that the whole of the space above the centre would be just for men. There were, after all, more men than women wanting to live in a community at that time. The centre would – obviously – be open to everyone, and women could establish communities elsewhere.

This sudden change was controversial; many of the women were deeply unhappy, feeling that they'd been marginalized from the project. Some of the men were against the idea too. Tensions between men and women, and a certain distrust of the single-sex idea, arose again. It provoked heated debate among the fifty or so Order members who attended the third Order Convention in early 1976.

Sangharakshita repeatedly expressed his conviction that women could establish dynamic and vibrant situations of their own, and that to do so independently of men would be spiritually beneficial for them. He emphasized that they shouldn't fall into the trap of thinking that the men's projects were 'where it was at'.

A group of women decided to form a new community, called Amaravati. They would have a 'common purse' – sharing their income, and making a bold attempt to live communally. It would be a more practice-orientated, retreat-like situation, with a daily programme of meditation, work, yoga, and puja. This was a more radical and intensive approach to community living than had been tried in the past.

In the summer of 1977 they moved into a large house in Wanstead, east London. The renovation of dilapidated old buildings features frequently in the early history of the FWBO and here the young pioneers were at it again. As one of their team, Dhammadinna, described it:

> All the time we were up against our lack of skill and our unfamiliarity with hard physical labour, and there were often tears of frustration or rage as people

struggled with difficult and unfamiliar jobs ... The experience was at times frightening – there was no one to bail us out, to turn to, or to hand things over to – and often painful and explosive. It was also extremely liberating as we discovered that we could do the work ourselves and that we could live happily together ... and not only survive, but grow and develop.[72]

Dhammadinna went on to argue that it had been harder for them than the men: '... the move to Amaravati represented for women a much more radical change than did, say, the move to Sukhavati for men, as there was much more resistance and conditioning to overcome ...'[73] Women at that time could undervalue themselves, they could tend to let men always lead, and so be unused to taking initiative themselves. Consequently, the project had entailed an even more fundamental breakthrough, 'Basically, we had done what many feminists were doing, but with a spiritual rather than a political perspective.'[74]

Amaravati attracted women visitors from all over the FWBO and was a significant landmark in the development of the women's wing and the movement. Around the same time in the late 1970s, four women moved into a ramshackle collection of old farm buildings near Aslacton, 14 miles south of Norwich, and for a few years this became 'Mandarava', the first women's retreat centre.

However, it wasn't until the mid-1980s that a permanent retreat centre for women was established. Sanghadevi took a leading role, forming a charity to raise funds, and gradually moving the project forward, strongly encouraged by Sangharakshita. In 1983, there was a month-long retreat on a Scottish island attended by every single woman in the Order – all 21 of them (which was about 15% of the whole Order in the West at that time).[75] They discussed their vision for the new retreat centre. They decided to search for a property where they could hold retreats for 25 to 30 women, and would be able to cater for bigger numbers if necessary. The project generated excitement and anticipation throughout the whole movement. By 1985, they'd raised sufficient funds and a property was found. Cornhill Farm, on the border between north Shropshire, England and Wales, and the seven acres of land that surrounded the buildings, became Taraloka Retreat Centre. They moved in during November of that year and were running their first retreat by Christmas. In the next few years there were a number of building projects, overseen by Dayanandi, a qualified architect, who became chair of the retreat centre after Sanghadevi. One week they'd be running a meditation retreat, the next they'd be out converting a barn, removing concrete cattle troughs with pneumatic drills. The facilities improved, the number of retreats held there steadily increased, and Taraloka attracted women from all over the world.[76]

The women's wing was now gaining real strength and momentum. From 1986 until 2002 they had their own magazine – *Dakini*, later published as *Lotus Realm*. A women's ordination team had formed and started fundraising for their own ordination training retreat centre. This led to the opening of Tiratanaloka in the Brecon Beacons, South Wales in 1992. The ordination team there worked under considerable pressure: there were now hundreds of women who'd asked for ordination, but still relatively few women Order members at centres to help them. (At this time, about 29% of Order members, excluding India, were women.) This increased the burden on the central ordination team. But it has been a huge success story. There were about 100 women Order members when Tiratanaloka opened in 1992; by 2009 there were more than 500. Women are now being ordained in larger numbers than men, and, on current trends, the women's and men's wings in the Order will even out numerically in 2014.

Meanwhile, in 2000, the Aranya project (Sanskrit for 'wilderness' or 'forest') was launched. This was an appeal for funds for a wild and beautiful place for longer retreats for women, including ordination retreats. The fundraising was conducted with a degree of professionalism and expertise hitherto unseen in the FWBO, and it met its target. But finding a suitable location proved to be much harder. For a time, it looked like property prices were going up so fast that the money raised would be inadequate, and they'd almost be back at square one again. But, eventually, land was purchased in Spain, followed by another challenging building project. The area is isolated, mountainous, and with stunning views of the surrounding landscape. They'd discovered that 'Aranya' meant 'spider' in Spanish, and 'Aranyaloka' would have translated as something like 'crazy spider', so they needed to find a new name for the retreat centre. It became Akashavana, 'a forest retreat of luminous space', and the first ordination retreat was held there in 2007.

◈

Not only did separate men's and women's retreat facilities develop, but by the 1980s, communities, businesses, study groups, and Order events were organized on a single-sex basis too. Most people's experience was that this was more helpful, avoiding complex and potentially messy dynamics around sexual attraction and projection. It gave people the opportunity to be with just their own gender, who were likely to understand one another's spiritual needs, and with whom genuine friendship and communication could perhaps more easily develop. Many people's experience was that single-sex activities were just simpler, easier, and more enjoyable.

But the old tensions were still there. Sometimes the single-sex idea could be applied in an immature way. What began as a relatively healthy, youthful freeing of oneself from one's unrealistic ideas about the other sex sometimes spilled over into the expression of harsh, dismissive ideas about them. Men at public centres, working hard against their tendency to get romantically involved with women, sometimes veered too far to the other extreme, and became cold and unfriendly towards them. Sometimes the only woman Order member in a particular city wouldn't be allowed to join the local Order chapter, as the men in it wanted to keep it single-sex, and she would be left feeling isolated and alone. By no means did these things always happen, but there were times when women experienced themselves as unwelcome intruders into a predominantly male world.

At Windhorse:Evolution, structures also developed along single-sex lines, except that – as it was such a large organization – it was inevitable that men and women would be working together in the same location. The single-sex idea was applied as rigorously as possible within these constraints, with separate work-teams, and even separate dining facilities. But increasingly, people felt it was actually producing *less* healthy relations between men and women. 'The whole culture didn't conduce to the development of sensible adult relationships between the sexes,' writes one ex-employee. 'Being partially separated yet still around each other could lead to extreme projection.'[77]

All this was exacerbated by an agreement among the male and female staff at Windhorse:Evolution's base in Cambridge that they wouldn't enter into sexual relationships with others in the business. This dated back to 1989 when Windhorse had an all-male workforce and many of the men were teaching at the new Cambridge Buddhist Centre. They felt it would be inappropriate to get involved with women who were new to the Buddhist centre, and so made the agreement among themselves, as a way of being clear and ethical. As Windhorse:Evolution expanded, and as women came to work at the business, the agreement was extended. They wanted to create a workplace environment where simplicity and contentment was supported and encouraged. But as the years went on, and certainly by the late 1990s, it became clear that the situation was full of contradictions, especially as some people were exempt because they had been in relationships prior to the original agreement. More and more people disagreed with the policy and felt they weren't being treated like adults, free to make their own decisions. Eventually, it simply fell apart.

This mirrored a change in single-sex activities throughout the FWBO. When the idea emerged, the FWBO had been a predominantly young and inexperienced sangha. But in an older – and hopefully more mature – community, people felt they didn't need to apply the idea so severely, nor did they want an FWBO culture that was so strongly prescriptive. According to Vishvapani:

> At the Croydon Buddhist Centre, it was applied with astonishing rigidity: men and women working just a few feet apart would avoid eye contact, and sometimes go for months barely exchanging a word. Over the years, in my experience, understanding of single-sex practice has become humanized, emphasizing the opportunities it offers for developing friendships, rather than aversion to the opposite sex.'78

A more relaxed practice of single-sex activities has emerged. They are still seen as valuable – even crucial – while it is acknowledged that there can be healthy and helpful relationships between the sexes too. In the recent Order survey, over 80% of respondents still valued single-sex situations.

Taking the long view, we can see that two vibrant wings, men's and women's, have emerged in the FWBO. Each wing has a growing experience and understanding of their own spiritual needs, ways of practising the spiritual life, and how to develop as fully-rounded human beings. The single-sex idea ensures that both men and women are in positions of autonomy, responsibility, and leadership. Both wings have much-loved facilities in the UK and Europe. Padmaloka is a central focus for the men's wing. For many years it has had a strong and harmonious community, and a spiritually bracing, but friendly, atmosphere all of its own. Guhyaloka has magical associations for the many men who've been there to be ordained, or for solitary retreats. Taraloka is at the heart of the women's wing, running retreats for women of all levels of experience. It has twice recently been named the 'Retreat Centre of the Year' by the UK Good Retreat Guide. Akashavana and Tiratanaloka have also been obvious success stories.

The biggest source of controversy on gender issues was a book published in 1995. Written by Subhuti, *Women, Men, and Angels*[79] was an explanation of Sangharakshita's views on the relative aptitude of men and women for the spiritual life. The book argued that women's biological conditioning made it harder for them to tread the earlier stages of the path to Enlightenment; for women, there was – at least initially – more conditioning to overcome.

It maintained that Sangharakshita based these ideas on definite precedents in the Buddhist tradition, along with his own observation.[80] He wanted people to be aware of his views and to give them consideration because he felt they would help both men and women to work constructively with their basic biological conditioning. He was concerned that they looked at their conditioning from a Buddhist point of view, and not just in terms of contemporary popular opinions and mores. However, the book made it clear that they did not have to agree with his opinion.[81] What was of overriding importance was that he taught (again following the Buddhist tradition) that both men and women could gain

Enlightenment. Subhuti, too, wanted himself and others in the Order to be open and honest about their teacher's views, and to give them a fair hearing.

The book was highly contentious. In the wider Buddhist world, it gained the FWBO a reputation for being 'anti-women'. It caused huge discussion and debate within the movement too. Many people accepted its perspective. The 'facts' did seem to support the theory; at that time, more men than women were being ordained and it appeared easier for the men. A lot of people so looked up to Sangharakshita that they thought he must be right. Some women Order members liked *Women, Men, and Angels*, and welcomed the challenge to make more spiritual effort. There was a series of films and books about women's approach to the spiritual life that were made partly in response to the book.

Not everyone agreed; there was intermittent debate in *Shabda* (the Order newsletter), and Subhuti received letter after letter criticizing the book. Some people found its confrontational, polemical style discouraging. Others read it as advocating a biological determinism. Buddhism is not, of course, deterministic, but teaches that all of our conditioning can eventually be overcome. In fact, the book did make this point, clearly distinguishing 'determinism' from 'conditioning'.[82] Others disagreed more strongly, disputing the idea that women's conditioning was disadvantageous, or the extent to which our conditioning is biological, rather than social and cultural. A few women Order members even cited *Women, Men, and Angels* as a reason for deciding to resign from the Order.

Eventually, in 2003, Subhuti – who was clearly upset that the book helped lead to the resignation of some people from the Order – wrote to *Shabda* to qualify what he'd originally said.

> I regret that the article was published in the way that
> it was, giving it an official weight and authority. It

seems obvious to me now that it would have been far better if it had circulated as an informal pamphlet or appeared in Articles *Shabda*, as I had originally intended.[83]

He had also come to the conclusion that it was difficult, if not impossible, to measure spiritual aptitude. It wasn't like running a 100-metre race, or testing someone's IQ. How could you measure subtle, inner qualities such as wisdom or compassion?

This statement was welcomed in the Order and matched where many people had themselves arrived with the issue. It was helpful to be aware that as a man, or as a woman, one would have a certain cultural, psychological, and biological conditioning. But it was not helpful, or necessary, to make comparisons *between* men and women. The book, and most of the ensuing debate, only discussed problematic aspects of women's conditioning, whereas *both* men and women needed to understand the particular conditioning they were working with.

Only 10% of women Order members and 25% of men Order members now say they agree with *Women, Men, and Angels*, according to a recent survey.[84] Some regret that originally they had gone along with it – promoting and defending the ideas at FWBO centres. For them, it has been a painful lesson in thinking for oneself, in listening with respect and receptivity to your teacher, trying to understand *why* they might be telling you something, but not automatically agreeing with everything they say.

There has been a positive side to the FWBO's discourse on men and women. Becoming more aware of gender conditioning has been helpful to many people, as has the FWBO's caution about certain aspects of feminism. While feminism enabled women to make huge, positive strides forward, other strands of it have been criticized in the FWBO – such as when, for example, the 'masculine' is devalued, or when hierarchy is seen as inherently oppressive. Many men and women in the FWBO have found a critique of these views helpful, refreshing, and liberating.

It is hugely significant that the movement that published *Women, Men, and Angels* is also the movement whose teacher was among the first to ordain women in the West. Not only that; as we'll explore more fully in Chapter 8, he set up an Order in which men's and women's ordinations are of equal status, and in which women ordain other women. Perhaps even more radically, this also applies to the Order in the much more 'traditional' society of India. There, too, there is a thriving women's wing.

7
Many Cultures, One Community

The FWBO was the first of the UK-born Buddhist movements to spread beyond its own shores. In 1971 an Order member named Aksobhya emigrated to New Zealand, and started running classes in Auckland. A year later Vajrabodhi and Bodhisri, who had also gotten involved in the FWBO in London, went back to their homeland –Finland – and began Buddhist activities there. In 1974 Sangharakshita made his first visit to Finland, and, later in the year, to New Zealand, where he conducted a number of ordinations – the first outside the UK. Over the years Sangharakshita was to spend much of his time travelling to overseas FWBO centres and groups, giving encouragement and inspiration.

From that time on, the FWBO gradually expanded into other countries. Sometimes this seemed to happen almost by chance, for example when (as we saw in Chapter 4) Lokamitra turned up in Nagpur on the very day of the twenty-first anniversary of the mass conversion of Dalits to Buddhism. At other times, Order members sought adventure, the chance to trail-blaze, and take the Dharma to a new land. Though there was never a blueprint for the growth of the FWBO, expansion was strongly encouraged. Sometimes there were more planned projects, in which a small team would move to a new country together.

Although, from one perspective, the rate of growth was remarkable, it wasn't as fast as the rapid expansion of the movement in the UK and India. By its twenty-first birthday, the FWBO had 16 centres in the UK, eight in India, but only ten in the whole of the rest of the world. These ten were located in just eight countries: New Zealand, Finland, Australia, Germany, Holland, Spain, Sweden, and the USA. Establishing an FWBO centre in a new culture was perhaps more difficult than doing so in the UK.

The first thing to contend with was the practical business of getting by. When Varadakini arrived, clutching her suitcase, at Paris Gare du Nord in August 1997, she was returning to her native land, but it was still tough making ends meet:

> From a cheap hotel room, with no telephone, no cooking facilities, I struggled to open a bank account when to do so I needed proof of address, and find a permanent address when to do so I needed a bank account... I was alone there and nobody to anybody. No established centre ... or fellow Order members to back me up or hide behind ...[85]

Those who'd landed in a new country faced the challenge of learning a different language. As Paramacitta found when she moved to Valencia, Spain in 1992:

> Language was perhaps the biggest and most painful cultural barrier to cross ... I was often trying to communicate complex ideas or personal impressions

with an imperfect grasp of which words I should be using, which sometimes led to gigantic misunderstandings…. It is like growing up all over again: learning to speak, facing the humiliation of making ridiculous mistakes so that people laugh at you or look at you with total incomprehension on their faces.[86]

Then there are the obvious – and not so obvious – cultural differences to get to know and understand. When Moksananda went to teach in Spanish-speaking countries, he learned that people from other cultures weren't necessarily going to do things according to his expectations:

In Britain there is a 'tradition' for people on retreats to go for walks in *pairs*, as a way of deepening communication. I remember how odd it seemed to me, on my first retreat in Mexico, to see groups of *three*, *four*, even *five* retreatants (on one occasion *twenty*!) setting off together. Nevertheless, they seemed to be getting to know each other very well![87]

Moving to a new country might mean that the nearest FWBO centre was hundreds, even thousands, of miles away. There would be scant resources to draw on: fewer Dharma books had been translated and published, and there would be no FWBO communities, Buddhist businesses or retreat centres. As Paramacitta discovered, it all depended on just one or two people to communicate and embody the Dharma:

The FWBO is a complex thing, difficult to describe to people without reference to existing institutions such as those that exist in the UK. There, the principles and practices are well established and people can see how they work; they can meet others who live the life. In Spain there was just us, trying to convey the infinite variety of the FWBO.[88]

For her, it was:

… the most spiritually fulfilling, as well as the most frustrating and at times painful experience of my life … I am more convinced than ever of the need to make connections with people across all boundaries, to break down the social and cultural barriers that divide us…. I can see how the experience here has … forced me to go deeper in my understanding of the Dharma … I wouldn't change that for an easy life.[89]

In its first 21 years the FWBO established centres in ten countries, and in the next 20 years it took the Dharma to another 15. The FWBO has gradually become a worldwide community of Dharma practitioners. They live in very different cultures, speak different languages, and yet share a particular approach to the Buddhist path. How is it possible, in one short chapter, to convey the richness and diversity of this community? It is obviously not possible to give a potted history of each centre in every country. Instead, this chapter tells the story of just six people who have taught, or who are teaching, the Dharma beyond the UK, one from each populated continent of the globe: Africa, North America, South America, Asia, Australasia and Europe, to give a glimpse of the internationality of the FWBO, and a sense of how the Dharma is applicable to many different cultures and situations. There are many more tales that deserve to be told. Hopefully, local FWBO centres will ensure those stories are recorded and not forgotten.

❧

Vajradhara had been involved with the London Buddhist Centre since the mid-1990s after coming to the UK from Durban, South Africa in 1985. He left South Africa in order to avoid military service during the closing years of the apartheid era. He'd seen through the system of apartheid, and, growing up a gay man, he was also disillusioned with Christianity and its attitude to sexuality. He was a staunch campaigner for many social and political issues: anti-apartheid, nuclear disarmament, human rights, gay liberation, ecology, animal welfare, and HIV/AIDS. But he knew from his own experience how easily campaigning for change could slip into self-righteous rage. He realized he also wanted to change his own mind and heart, and that was what brought him to the Dharma.

He went back regularly to visit his parents in South Africa and in 1997, having heard there was now an Order member living there, he decided to look her up. Ratnajyoti was a German woman who'd gone to live in Johannesburg in the early 1990s when her husband got a job at the university. Even before she was ordained, she had started running classes in Buddhism and meditation, in addition to having a full-time job as a nursery school teacher. But it was not easy to keep an FWBO group running when you were so isolated from the rest of the FWBO. She and Vajradhara formed a friendship, and he realized that he could help.

In 2001, just nine months after being ordained, Vajradhara started going to teach the Dharma in South Africa. The plan was that he'd go for six months each year. He met a man named Wayne Sampson, they began a relationship, and Wayne, who'd had a longstanding interest in meditation, got involved in FWBO Buddhist practice. He became one of the driving forces behind the development of the centre in Johannesburg. In 2004, he found two adjacent shops for lease; he used one as his hairdressing salon and the other was used for Buddhist classes. Grants from the 'growth fund' of Windhorse:Evolution, the Buddhist business back in the UK, were crucial in getting them going. Then they saw a house for sale across the road from the shop and decided to try to buy it for the Buddhist centre.

They were outbid for the house, but the owners had been to the Buddhist centre, and so told them that if they could match the bid, and do it quickly, the house was theirs. A two-week scramble to arrange loans and mortgages ensued, and they got the property. It was a financial stretch and only happened thanks to the generosity of Vajradhara, Wayne, and others.

At last they had a public Buddhist centre, with their own facilities, and a dedicated shrine space. The Johannesburg Centre, the first FWBO centre on African soil, opened in 2006.[90] It is in a leafy suburb of the city and has its own garden – a green, beautiful, and calm oasis. They named it 'Shantikula', which they translate as 'peaceful tribe'. The Buddha figure on the shrine depicts the Buddha as an African man. They were taking the first steps in translating the Dharma into a form appropriate for the social and cultural conditions of Africa.

Vajradhara continued to spend six months of every year there, experimenting and learning how the Dharma might take root in African soil. Although South Africa is a beautiful and, in many ways, wealthy country, there is still a negative legacy left by apartheid. It is a deeply conservative culture, with strong strands of cynicism. It is a society in a state of fear of the 'other', and particularly a huge fear of violent crime. Many people won't travel far, or venture out at night time, and houses are typically surrounded by electric fences, with window bars and alarm systems. Vajradhara sees part of his role as exemplifying fearlessness. For example, he'll deliberately go out of the centre compound at night to see people to their cars and say goodbye to them. 'Be prudent, but fearless' is what he tries to communicate. The centre has a steady stream of people of all colours, and he also tries to cross barriers by spending time with their cleaner, gardener, and car guard. He sees the work as a long-term project, trying to plant a few seeds of trust and togetherness in a still divided and fearful country.

Vajradhara's connection to the wider FWBO community is important to him. Even though it is thousands of miles away, he feels a positive sense of being 'held to account' that helps sustain his practice of altruism. At the same time, he feels free to communicate the Dharma in the way appropriate for their situation, to be 'independent without having to reinvent the wheel'.

In 2008 Vajradhara's health took a turn for the worse and he had to return to the UK for treatment. At the time of writing, he is very seriously ill in hospital in London. Ratnajyoti has also had to leave South Africa for Europe. The fledgling Centre in Johannesburg is in a precarious state again. On the positive side, Wayne was ordained in September 2009 and received the name Achalaraja.

In 1990 Lisa Cullen, an American woman in her 20s, was travelling round Asia. She found herself increasingly drawn to the Buddhists she saw on her travels. As she was later to describe it:

> ... while I sat gazing at the gentle gold Buddhas of Thailand, faith arose in me.... I had been travelling around Asia for many months, and wherever I saw Buddhists, wearing robes or with kesas around their necks, I knew I wanted what they had. Rather I wanted to be in some way how they were ...[91]

She attended a retreat led by a Tibetan monk in Kathmandu. His English was rudimentary, his accent thick, and she found it hard to understand him. Then she came across a Westerner running an introductory class. His name was Amoghacitta and he was from the FWBO. He was explaining the Wheel of Life in a way that was clear and accessible. She learned to meditate and became vegetarian.

However, back home in San Francisco, it was hard to sustain the fragile momentum of her Buddhist practice. Only later did Lisa discover there were FWBO activities getting going in her area. After attending a retreat led by Karunadevi, she gradually got involved. The first centre opened in a storefront in the Sunset area of the city. Then, in 1993, Paramananda and Paramabodhi arrived from the UK and the following year a new centre was established in the Mission District, a culturally diverse region of the city. The two Order members lived on the first floor while Lisa and a friend moved into the second.

Paramananda and Paramabodhi were in the US on a religious visa, and since the centre was small and finances precarious, they lived on $60 per week without medical insurance. Their style was 'super casual', i.e. avoiding administration as much as possible. Lisa bonded strongly with Paramananda, and in 1994 asked to be ordained into the Western Buddhist Order. The ordination training process was still in its early days in the USA. The first retreat was in someone's house in Seattle; after that she needed to travel to Aryaloka Retreat Center, which was on the east coast – 3000 miles away.

Then she came across a commentary on the *Sutra of Golden Light* by Sangharakshita. In it, he put forward views about the relative aptitudes of men and women for the spiritual life, views that were later expounded by Subhuti in the book *Women, Men, and Angels*.[92] This hit her, as she was to describe it, with the force of a runaway train. For a couple of years, she struggled with her response to what she felt were deeply negative views of women. How could a Buddhist teacher hold such views? Why did members of the Order go along with it?

Eventually, she decided to leave and withdrew her request for ordination. But it was a painful departure. As she wrote in her journal at the time:

> I withdrew my request for ordination yesterday. It feels now like, say, I was caught in a trap so I had to chew off my leg in order to free myself. My leg which is gone now is a bunch of people who had become a part of me and with whom I have severed a supremely sweet kind of contact.[93]

Lisa tried other Buddhist groups, but realized that wherever she went, there would be a mixture of good and bad things that she would agree and disagree with.

> I could have become a Wiccan or a Sufi and forgotten the whole matter, but I am a Buddhist. A Buddhist who was unwilling to start over, and after looking long and hard into the matter, saw no reason to. In fact, saw great reason not to. Practising Western Buddhism is the only way I have discovered as yet to be happy, to feel that the actions of my life have any meaning, shining a tiny clear light into a miasmic world.[94]

Although she still strongly objected to the views, she also saw that women were not discriminated against in the FWBO. Quite to the contrary; it was a good place to practice. She went back, renewed her request for ordination, and was ordained at Tuscany in 2001, receiving the name Suvarnaprabha.

By this time, the woman with whom she had moved into the Centre had been ordained. Viveka, a Chinese-American woman, was also to become chair of the centre after Paramananda and

Paramabodhi returned to the UK. Viveka had been a consultant to community organizations, and she was able to bring these skills into the sangha, as well as engaging in outreach work to make meditation and Dharma available to people of colour. Suvarnaprabha joined her as director of the centre, teaching many of the classes and organizing a programme of arts events.

These days, the San Francisco Buddhist Center is one of the two largest FWBO centres in the USA. (The other large centre is Aryaloka on the east coast. There are a number of smaller centres across the country, especially down the east coast, and in Canada too.) The San Francisco Buddhist Center has a particularly strong emphasis on collective meditation practice. Five mornings per week, people gather at the centre to meditate before going to work. Each January, the usual programme of activities is suspended to make way for a month-long 'rainy season retreat'. Some people join in for the whole programme, others drop in when they can.

Life is busy in America; economic security, pensions, and medical insurance are big concerns for people. People work hard, long hours. It is much harder to get time off for retreats than it is in the UK, or to find space for Buddhist practice, and so their presentation of the Dharma has to take this into account. It also makes Suvarnaprabha feel grateful for her job at the San Francisco Buddhist Center, because she can take time off for retreats and her work is closely connected to her Buddhist practice.

Antonio Perez grew up in the remote Venezuelan countryside, and yet, for reasons he cannot explain, he found himself drawn to Buddhism. He always felt a strange sense of having been thrown into an unfamiliar world, and of needing to find his way back to where he'd been before. There were programmes on TV which fascinated him; they showed Tibetan monks chanting magical mantras, or Zen monks meditating in the snow. In his late teens, he found a book on Zen and martial arts at a bus terminal, took it home, and learned to meditate from it.

He went to Caracas University and, when offered the chance of a scholarship to finish his degree at Manchester University, he took the opportunity. He arrived in England in October 1978; he remembers the sun seeming oddly cool and low in the sky. Antonio kept up his studies, but really he was looking for training in the spiritual life. He read all sorts of spiritual and personal growth books, those of Erich Fromm making a particular impression.

One day, he wandered into the TV room at the university to find a young Turkish man watching a programme on alternative medicine. The man asked Antonio if he wanted to change the channel, assuming that the programme wouldn't appeal to him. But Antonio said it looked interesting, they got talking, and his new friend told him about the Manchester Buddhist Centre.

In 1980 he started attending classes at the centre, where Ratnaguna and Suvajra were doing most of the teaching. Later he was to meet Sangharakshita. On one level, the meeting was very everyday and ordinary; on another level, he felt that he had met his teacher. When his university course finished, he realized he wanted to stay in the UK and get more involved in the FWBO.

He ended up at the Croydon Buddhist Centre, working at Hockneys Restaurant. Here was a band of idealistic young people living a highly committed life, almost as though they were in a monastery. It was hard, but he stuck at it, and asked for ordination. He wrote to Sangharakshita telling him he'd found the focused, dedicated training he was looking for, and that he now wanted to make the best use of it, in order to prepare to go back to Venezuela one day. Sangharakshita replied to his letter and encouraged him.

In 1984 he was ordained, receiving the name Manjunatha. A few years later Manjunatha became the local men's Mitra convenor, and he was to play a key role in the 'Croydon Revolution' – questioning and challenging the unhealthy dynamic that had developed there, and helping to bring about change.[95]

Some years later, he went to see Sangharakshita, who asked him, 'Have you forgotten Latin America?' He decided it was now time to return, and the following year – 1992 – he flew back to Venezuela. He didn't really know what he was going to do there; he had been so busy in the restaurant at Croydon that he didn't actually have that much experience of teaching.

Luckily, help came in the form of Vajranatha, an English Order member who was fluent in Spanish. He visited Manjunatha and decided to move there and work with him for six months. Vajranatha then visited the city of Mérida, fell in love with it, and felt it was the right place to found a centre. Mérida is the fourth or fifth largest city in Venezuela, home to the University of the Andes, with a population of around a third of a million. It is situated on a high altitude river plain, and behind it lay Pico Boliva, the country's highest mountain. They thought it an attractive city, a good place to live.

Very quickly, they rented a flat in the city centre and classes got going. Manjunatha was worried nobody would come, but between ten and thirty people attended beginners' classes, and up to sixty could turn up for a day retreat. Vajranatha did much of the teaching in the early days; he was an accomplished teacher, while Manjunatha was still finding his feet.

Vajranatha's six-month visit turned into eight years, with him co-establishing the Centro Budista de Mérida and the associated men's community, and also buying for them the house in which these were based. Eventually, he moved on, and passed the baton to Manjunatha.

It is vital to Manjunatha to come back to the UK every year or two to reconnect with the FWBO and Order there. He says he 'forgets' what it means to be an Order member and needs to tune in to it again. Through meeting a few Order members, it is as if he is linked in with the whole Order and what it represents.

Others from the Centro Budista de Mérida have come to the UK to prepare for ordination; there are currently two people in training while working at Windhorse:Evolution. Manjunatha hopes that once they feel they've had sufficient training, they will return, so that the Dharma can be further established in their land.

❧

As we've seen in a previous chapter, the FWBO's main presence in Asia is in India, though there are also activities in Sri Lanka. But this next story is about an Order member venturing into the Chinese-speaking world.

Dhammaloka is a long-standing German Order member who, in the early 1980s, was co-founder of the Essen Centre, the first FWBO centre in Germany. He currently lives in the UK and works for Dharmapala College, running seminars and study retreats.

In 1995 he went travelling for two months in China, forming some good friendships along the way, and falling in love with the country. The landscape was varied and beautiful, and Chinese culture made a strong impact on him. Despite the turbulence of their country's recent history, the Chinese still had a highly developed sense of tradition and culture. It was so unlike anything he had experienced before; the contrasts in culture were more pronounced than, say, between the West and India. Dhammaloka was fascinated by some of those differences. In Europe, he would think of himself as being relatively reserved, yet here people told him he was very emotional in temperament. There was less individualism than in the West, people experiencing and identifying themselves much more through relationships and social connections.

Dhammaloka also saw that, although many people still had a positive connection with Buddhism, it needed re-presenting for the modern society that had come into being, so that it remained relevant to the busy, urbanized lives people were leading. He also sensed people's fear that Western consumerist values would destroy the old culture. In many ways, he shared their concern, though he didn't want it to lead to a polarization between East and West. He started to wonder if he could, in a small way, build bridges between people in these two different cultures, and also show how Buddhism could be renewed for the contemporary world.

He started learning Chinese, which he says is not as difficult as people in the West might think. Although he found some of the sounds difficult, the grammatical structure was clear and straight-forward for him. In 1998 he started travelling regularly to China, Malaysia, and Singapore, and running Buddhist activities.

A tiny, yet densely populated, island city-state at the southern tip of the Malay Peninsula, Singapore is a highly cosmopol-itan city. Most of the population is Buddhist, although there are also large numbers of Christians, Muslims and Taoists, as well as people with no religious affiliation. The head monk of the Buddhist Library there was very friendly towards Dhamm-aloka and the FWBO. However, Dhammaloka found it a hectic city, where people were relentlessly busy. There were also many Buddhist organizations already established there, and he decided to focus his efforts elsewhere.

Malaysia, another former British colony in the region, holds Islam, practised by 60% of the population, as its state religion. However, approximately 20% of the population is Chinese Buddhist. Dhammaloka discovered that in some quarters Sang-harakshita was already quite well known and respected. There was genuine interest in how the FWBO was developing a path of practice for a busy, contemporary world. He also found that many of the young people knew much more about Christianity than Buddhism. In a shopping centre in Malacca, he saw a well-run, well-resourced shop run by evangelical Christians. Down the road was a tiny, dusty Buddhist shop selling a few candles and some incense – reflecting that an old tradition badly needed to learn how to re-communicate itself and its values. Dhammaloka had the sense that this would be a good place for the FWBO to start a centre.

During visits to Malaysia, Dhammaloka is very active, giving talks, seminars, and meditation teaching. He may, for example, run a course that takes place every evening for a week – allowing him to give people as much input as possible in a short space of time. In the city of Malacca, he stays with a Mitra, Dr. Seet Boon Chong, whose help is crucial to keeping the activities going.

The situation in China is very different. Despite being repressed under Communist rule, Buddhism is now reviving, although very much along the traditional monk–lay lines. Dhammaloka mostly goes to stay with Ruan Yin Hua, a Mitra friend in Beijing, and runs courses in mindfulness under a more 'secular' guise. There is a Chinese Buddhist Association that approves and accredits any Buddhist activity, and, since Dhammaloka is visiting only briefly, getting accreditation would be complicated and time-consuming. So for now, he works by other means, sensing again and again the great potential for Buddhism to renew itself in today's China.

Dhammaloka hopes to keep going with this work, though money is an issue for him; he needs to cover his airfares and living costs while travelling. He wonders what the best approach will be. Perhaps in some locations FWBO centres could be established; perhaps in others it would be more fruitful to get into dialogue with the already existing Buddhist organizations and tell them what the FWBO has learned about making the Dharma available in the contemporary world. He finds this encounter between the FWBO and traditional Buddhist cultures fascinating and exciting.

❦

Vaughan Baguley was a young man living in south London in the 1970s who travelled extensively, including making several overland trips to Australia. He explored widely in the spiritual world, travelling to India and Thailand and reading such books as the *Tibetan Book of the Dead*, the *Bhagavad Gita*, and the *Kabbalah*. Despite all this ranging about, he hadn't yet found a path to follow. Then he came across 'Vision and Transformation', a series of audio tapes by Sangharakshita on the Buddha's Eightfold Path. Here, he realized, was a practical path that he could pursue, that would give his spiritual aspirations a more definite direction.

He went along to the FWBO centre in Purley, south London. Vaughan was a fiercely independent man, suspicious of 'groups'. He stood in a phone box just over the road from the centre and watched carefully who came and went. Feeling too shy and nervous to go in, he then went home again. But the next week, he went back and made it into the class. He was befriended by Nagabodhi and a year later, in 1977, he'd quit his job, was living in the local men's community, and was helping to establish the Secret Garden Café, one of the new cooperative businesses forming at that time.

Vaughan was ordained in 1979, receiving the name Dharmamati. Only a month or two later, he was approached by Dipankara, an Australian Order member who wanted to establish the FWBO 'down under'. They'd had the idea of forming small teams of pioneers; Manjuvajra was forming a team to go to the USA, and Dipankara was doing the same for Australia. He'd heard that Dharmamati had been to Australia; would he be interested in joining him and Buddhadasa? Dharmamati immediately thought: 'Yes!'

In 1981 he arrived in Sydney and formed a men's community along with Dipankara, Vipula (an Order member who'd moved over from New Zealand), and Dave Rice (who would be ordained as Jayaghosa). Rosemary Sharples (who later became Cittaprabha) and Vajrasuri were also important figures in those early days.

They ran their first meditation day retreat that winter. About ten people turned up; there seemed to be interest, and they carried on. It didn't seem right to name a converted bedroom in a house something as grand as the 'Sydney Buddhist Centre', so instead they called themselves 'The Sydney Meditation Community'. By 1986, however, they'd raised enough money to rent the top floor of a three-storey building. Dipankara and Dharmamati did much of the renovation work, and now they had their own Buddhist centre.

Looking back on those early days, Dharmamati says he was never homesick; instead, he felt a sense of adventure and excitement in bringing the FWBO to a new land. It required considerable self-motivation; it could be hard to keep going when the rest of the FWBO was so far away. Even New Zealand, where the FWBO was more established, was a three-hour flight away. He found Australians more outspoken than the British. Discussion groups could be livelier; people weren't afraid to ask awkward questions. This could be challenging, but it was also stimulating and enjoyable.

A time of self-doubt and difficulty came in 1989 when he split up with his girlfriend. He was heartbroken, yet felt he had to continue with his work as chair of the Sydney Centre. The tension created by pushing himself to do this eventually became unbearable. Dharmamati moved away to the Blue Mountains, west of Sydney, and later Cittaprabha became the chair of the centre. The idea was for Dharmamati to live there for six months to recover, but he ended up staying for 11 years.

Though only two hours from Sydney, the Blue Mountains boast huge, ancient red sandstone cliffs and canyons forested with eucalyptus trees. These sometimes emit a vapour that creates a blue haze, which gives the area its name. Dharmamati ran classes in the area, and eventually there was a small men's community there. Meanwhile, the Sydney sangha, which Dharmamati continued to visit, carried on developing. They now had a retreat centre – Vijayaloka – on the edge of the city, where the suburbs give way to the Australian bush. Buddhadasa and Guhyavajra were also establishing a centre in Melbourne. Then, in the late 1990s, Dharmamati returned to Sydney to help renovate another property so that the centre could move to a location right in the centre of the city. He then stayed on and worked there as a Dharma teacher.

In 2006 his life entered another phase; he came back to the UK to work as Sangharakshita's secretary. Dharmamati says he feels privileged to have helped Sangharakshita in this way, and to have the opportunity to spend more time with him. Retiring from that role in 2009, Dharmamati still wants to be around for Sangharakshita for as long as he is needed, though one day he may return to Australia.

❧

In the late 1990s, Michal Balik was a student from Poland studying at the university in Frankfurt (Oder), a small town on the German side of the border between the two countries. He went along to the Berlin FWBO Centre where Dayaraja taught him to meditate, and he immediately knew he'd found his path: 'I need to dig', he thought, 'but at least I know where to dig.'

Dayaraja suggested that Michal could help get some classes going in Frankfurt. He liked the idea that he could be *involved* right from the start. He organized the classes and Anomarati came down from Berlin to teach once a week.

In 2000, having finished university and wanting to get more involved in the FWBO, Michal came to the UK and worked at

Friends Organic, one of the businesses associated with the London Buddhist Centre. On a return visit to Poland, he thought he'd go into a bookshop and see what books were available on Buddhism in his own language. A flyer which fell out of one of the books.gave a whole list of Buddhist books, one of which was *Buddhism Across the Ages* by Sangharakshita. Michal didn't know that Sangharakshita had been translated into Polish, so he phoned the publisher to buy a copy. He was told, however, that the book – a translation of *A Survey of Buddhism* – wasn't available. The publisher didn't have sufficient funds to print and distribute it.

Back in the UK, Michal wrote to Subhuti to ask if anyone could help get the book published. Subhuti passed the letter on to Sangharakshita, who offered to donate the necessary money. In May 2002, Michal and eleven others accompanied Sangharakshita on a trip to Poland. They met the publisher, Cezary Wozniak, who organized three book launches of the Polish *A Survey of Buddhism*. Sangharakshita gave talks, and Michal translated. It was clear that there was potential for the FWBO in Poland.

Through translating for Sangharakshita, Michal felt there had been 'a meeting of minds' and a friendship developed between them. The next year, he moved from London to Birmingham to look after Sangharakshita, who was at that time suffering from poor health. But gradually his health improved and their friendship deepened. In 2004 Michal was ordained, with Sangharakshita acting as his private preceptor and giving him the name Nityabandhu.

He and Amarasiddhi – who was half Polish and spoke the language well, and was also a key person in establishing activities in those early days – had been visiting Poland every few months. They 'parachuted into Poland', running meditation classes or weekend retreats. It wasn't easy organizing activities from a distance. The country still had a very strong Catholic culture and anything 'alternative' could be viewed with suspicion. Yet they also attracted young people who were looking for something different.

For a while they'd been thinking of moving there to found an FWBO centre, and Sangharakshita had offered to help fund a property, using money given by Windhorse:Evolution that he'd been asked to distribute. But which city should they go to? Amarasiddhi suggested Krakow rather than the capital Warsaw. Krakow was the second largest city in Poland, with about a million people, and a university. It was the only large Polish city not destroyed in the Second World War, and therefore had retained its beautiful old architecture. There is a river running through the city, with mountains visible in the distance. It was also where the publisher of Sangharakshita's book was based.

Property prices were rising at a phenomenal rate, so they wanted to buy quickly. In 2005 they purchased a place in the old Jewish Quarter of the city. One day not long afterwards, Nityabandhu was standing outside the property when an old lady came over from the building opposite and asked him what was going to be there. 'A club where people can meet', he said, worried that she'd be antagonistic to the idea of a Buddhist centre. 'What kind of people?' she asked. 'Buddhist', replied Nityabandhu. It turned out that she had moved to Krakow from Brighton, where for years she had rented a house to a FWBO Buddhist community. She even remembered Sangharakshita visiting Brighton in the 1970s.

Nityabandhu carried on living with Sangharakshita in Birmingham, and working as a civil servant to save money to go back to Poland. Eventually, in March 2008, he moved there and joined Shantika, another Pole, who had moved to Krakow in 2007. Nityabandhu's friend Karunabandhu, who was a builder, joined them to help with the renovation of the building. Another Order member, the late Mahananda, who was of Polish heritage, had generously donated funds for the work.

In July 2008, they were joined by Sassirika, a Chinese–British woman who had been ordained in 2006. It was harder for her to make the transition as she only spoke very basic Polish, had never lived in a foreign country, and was only newly ordained. However, she and Nityabandhu were in a relationship and they wanted to be together. They and Shantika rented a flat together, earning their living by teaching English.

In September 2008 the new centre opened, and Sangharakshita came to cut the ribbon. The centre was named 'Sanghaloka': 'the place of spiritual community'. Having only relatively recently won independence from Communist rule, and with the war and generations of foreign occupation before that, Polish people can be distrusting of authority and organization. Nityabandhu and the others are deliberately trying to create a centre that does not feel 'institutional' or 'official'. They want the ethos to be as informal and sociable as possible.

Most people who come along are in their twenties or thirties. They like the simplicity and practicality of what is offered. They admire the three Order members for finding a way to live the kind of lives they want; they are amazed that such freedom is possible. Nityabandhu hopes that this sense of possibility will catch on, and that more people will join them and help them with the work they are doing.

8
At the Heart of the Sangha

Fifteen men are meditating in the shrine-room of Guhyaloka, a retreat centre in a mountainous valley in southern Spain. Wearing simple, slate-blue robes, they sit with eyes softly closed, bodies still, breathing steady. Orange light flickers from the candles onto the white-tiled wall. Incense smoke spirals slowly upwards.

Then one of the men stands up, bows to the shrine, and steps outside, his face a mixture of excitement and seriousness. Outside, the night air is cool and clean and, in the dark, he has to pick his way carefully over the rough ground dotted with juniper, rosemary, and rock-rose. He takes a path lined with white stones that winds down through some pine trees and then veers left to an outcrop of rocks. At this point, the path divides, and he pauses.

It seems as if one path leads downwards and out of the valley. Looking in that direction, in the far distance, he can see the twinkling, beckoning lights of a Spanish seaside town. The other path leads upwards to a place that, although they've been living here for two months, no one has yet been to. He takes that path.

Some way on, behind more rocks and pine trees, there is a stupa made of stone and whitish plasterwork, and standing three or four metres high. The structure is broad at the base and tapers upwards, pointing to the moon in the clear sky. He approaches slowly and purposefully. At the base of the stupa is a tiny door. He kneels down on all fours, the gravel underneath making imprints on his palms. Hands slightly shaking, he manages to unfasten the door and clambers inside.

❧

Hundreds of people are crammed into the shrine-room of a retreat centre in India, rows and rows of jubilant, joyful faces – a sea of smiles and laughter. The applause resounds around the hall, the clapping getting louder and faster. The most delighted faces of all are in the front row – a line of women, some Indian, some Western. They are all wearing beautiful blue saris, and round their shoulders are shining white kesas.[96] Their friends, laughing mischievously, are throwing handfuls of whirling flower petals over them.

They have just been ordained during a simple but powerful ceremony. A few moments ago, kneeling in front of their preceptor, they publicly recited the refuges and ten precepts. Then, one by one, they came forward and their preceptor placed a kesa round their neck. Now the time has come for their new Buddhist names to be announced and explained to the expectant crowd.

❧

Our story so far has focused on the growth and development of the FWBO. At its heart is the Western Buddhist Order itself, now a worldwide community of nearly two thousand men and women. What unites them is a common orientation of their lives towards the Three Jewels, a shared commitment to practice, and a collective understanding of what that entails.

The ceremony whereby people join the Order comprises two parts. In the first, the private ordination, the ordinand goes alone to meet with his or her private preceptor. It is as if they are prepared to take this step all by themselves. The private preceptor is there as a witness, confirming for them that their 'Going for Refuge' – their commitment to the Buddha, Dharma, and Sangha – is genuine and effective. With them, they recite the refuges and ten precepts[97] and dedicate themselves to Go for Refuge for the rest of their life. Their preceptor gives them a Buddhist name that expresses something of their qualities and spiritual potential. They may also receive a special meditation practice.

Some days later there is the public ordination. Along with others who have just had their private ordination, there is another ceremony that may be attended by friends, family, and Order members who've come to support and celebrate. This time, in front of those assembled, the ordinees chant the refuges and precepts together. They don't only make the commitment alone; they make it with the support and comradeship of others. Finally they step forward one by one, bowing before the public preceptor, and a white kesa is placed around their neck. They have now joined the Western Buddhist Order. All that remains is for their new names to be announced.

In Asia, ordination is frequently monastic.[98] Very often the lay followers will be much more nominally Buddhist. They may go frequently to the temples and worship the Buddha, observe the five precepts, and act with great generosity towards the monastic sangha. But they are unlikely to meditate, to study Buddhism, go on retreat, or really think of their lives as orientated towards Enlightenment. In addition, although the Buddha did found an order of nuns, this order dwindled substantially over the centuries and full ordination in Asian Buddhism has become an almost male-only institution.[99]

But as Buddhism has come to the West, this situation has changed. Most of those seriously following Buddhism are not monks, but they may be deeply, existentially engaged with practice, and want it to pervade all areas of their lives. They may meditate every day, go on long retreats, start Buddhist groups and centres, or undertake a serious study of the Dharma. And both men and women have taken up the Buddhist life in this way.

This is how it is in the Western Buddhist Order. In fact, there has been a particularly thorough examination of the relationship between spiritual commitment and lifestyle, a critique of over-identification of the spiritual life with monasticism,[100] and exploration of the implications of doing things differently. Not only are people able to practise Buddhism while living a variety of lifestyles, but they can also do so fully, to the extent of joining a Buddhist order. Not only do women have access to the teachings but they receive exactly the same ordination as men.

This understanding has been expressed most succinctly as 'commitment primary, lifestyle secondary'. You need a lifestyle that enables you to follow through the spiritual commitment you've made; but it is the commitment – the Going for Refuge – that is first and foremost, that really defines you as a Buddhist, and unites you with others who've made a similar commitment.

Although these teachings on 'the primacy of Going for Refuge' and on a unified order for men and women may seem obvious and unremarkable, in the context of traditional Buddhism they are radical and daring. In his writings, Sangharakshita has been on guard against Buddhists in the West thinking of monastic ordination, the Bodhisattva vows, or Tantric initiations[101] as putting you more properly or powerfully on the spiritual path. He emphasizes the common Going for Refuge that is the essential element to all of them.[102] This important strand of his teaching has emerged over time, through his experience both of traditional Buddhism in India and of founding an order in the West.

❧

The first private ordinations of twelve men and women into the Western Buddhist Order took place in the little basement in Monmouth Street, London. While one person had their ceremony, the others stood in the shop upstairs, waiting their turn. The private ordinations were followed a few days later – on 7 April 1968 – by the public ordinations, which were held at hired premises (Centre House). Two Theravadin monks and two Zen priests were present for the occasion.

In those first years everything was rudimentary and experimental. Once someone had been around for a while and looked as if they were seriously interested, Sangharakshita would take them out for a walk and suggest they could be ordained. If they agreed, their ordination might take place a couple of weeks later. They often had very little idea of what it really signified. There were hardly any other Order members from whom to imbibe its spirit and significance. No one – apart from Sangharakshita – had any real experience of the Buddhist life. But they had to make a start somewhere. It is hardly surprising that most of those earliest Order members resigned or drifted away as the Order developed and it started to become more apparent what kind of commitment ordination entailed. Nevertheless, some of them played a crucial role in establishing the FWBO in those early days.

Those first twelve men and women were ordained as *upasakas* or *upasikas* – lay brothers or sisters. Sangharakshita gave a talk in which he explained the four grades of ordination he envisaged for the new movement, which were based on the traditional model. In addition to the lay ordination, there would be senior lay, Bodhisattva, and monastic ordinations. These represented an increasing degree of experience, understanding, and commitment.

As the Order grew, there were more upasaka and upasika ordinations. Gotami was ordained as a senior laywoman in 1973, and there was one Bodhisattva ordination – that of Aksobhya in New Zealand in 1974. However, Sangharakshita's thinking was evolving as the Order developed. First, he was realizing more firmly and clearly the 'primacy of Going for Refuge' and no longer wanted to distinguish lay, Bodhisattva, and monastic as different levels of ordination. Secondly, the new Order members tended to practise more wholeheartedly, and work more fully to spread the Dharma than would ever be expected of a lay brother or sister in Asia. This was causing most confusion in India, where people would come into contact with both traditional Buddhism and the new movement.

At an Order meeting in India in March 1982, Sangharakshita therefore proposed dropping the titles of upasaka or upasika and using instead *Dhammachari* or *Dhammacharini*. This was accepted, and soon the new nomenclature spread to the West (where the Sanskrit was used: *Dharmachari* or *Dharmacharini*). The term means to 'live, walk, or fare in the Dharma'; so it had the additional advantage of describing more fully what ordination was about. There were also traditional precedents for using the term in Buddhist texts such as the *Dhammapada*.[103]

In April 1988, on the twentieth anniversary of the founding of the Order, Sangharakshita presented a paper entitled 'The History of My Going for Refuge'.[104] It was the fullest and most significant statement yet of his belief in the primacy of Going for Refuge, and the implications of that for ordination and the spiritual life. It showed how his understanding had developed gradually, through experience of his own spiritual path, and what had been learned in the founding and growth of the Order.

He reflected further on the significance of those first ordinations:

> The twelve people who made up the Western Buddhist Order had 'taken' the Three Refuges and Ten Precepts from me ... and their understanding of the meaning of Going for Refuge coincided with mine, at least partly. Like one lamp lighting a dozen others, I had been able to share with them my realization of the absolute centrality of the act of Going for Refuge and henceforth that realization would find expression not in my life only but also in theirs. Not that the realization in question was something fixed and final. It could continue to grow and develop, and find expression in a hundred ways as yet unthought of.[105]

For Sangharakshita, the Order was that shared understanding of Going for Refuge. As more and more people tried to live out that understanding, and through the very process of sharing it with others, it would develop and deepen. They were journeying on the path of the Dharma together; the more people that travelled the path, the clearer the way was made for others to follow.

In the Order, said Sangharakshita, each person was trying to act as an individual – freely, creatively, and with self-awareness. Yet they were also trying to act together – in friendship and harmony, and with awareness of the whole Order. When they achieved this 'coincidence of wills', a new kind of consciousness would be experienced: 'This consciousness is not the sum total of the individual consciousnesses concerned, nor even a kind of collective consciousness, but a consciousness of an entirely different order.'[106] It was synergy on the ethical and spiritual level, a mutual lifting up into more and more inspired states of mind.

He reflected back on the early 1970s when he'd started suggesting that the image of the thousand-armed Avalokitesvara could represent the Order. To him this was not just an attractive symbol for the Order; it was something that could really be achieved.

And perhaps, at its best, in the Order that new level of consciousness can sometimes be glimpsed. Order members have sensed it in the charged atmosphere at the start of a public ordination, in the heightened atmosphere of the shrine-room at a large Order gathering, or in the energized atmosphere of a work project.

❧

But the 'shared understanding' that constitutes the Order doesn't happen by magic. Over the years there has been an emphasis on the Order gathering and meeting in order to create the trust, friendship and communication that allow understanding to be shared. As the Order developed, the various forums and contexts in which it met evolved too. Local Order members began to meet weekly in chapters. There were more occasional regional and national gatherings, and international conventions.

The first convention was held in 1974, in the living room of Aryatara, the community in Purley, and attended by 29 Order members. In 1978, 70 Order members came to the tenth anniversary convention. They had to hire a school in order to provide enough facilities and accommodation, and it was the first time that they had to split into groups for study sessions, rather than staying together. In recent years, biennial International Order Conventions have been attended by hundreds of people. They are the closest the Order comes to being in one place at one time.

In 2009 the International Convention took place at Bodh Gaya – the place of the Buddha's Enlightenment in India – for the first time. Being in India made it possible for many more Indian Order members to attend, as well as Order members from

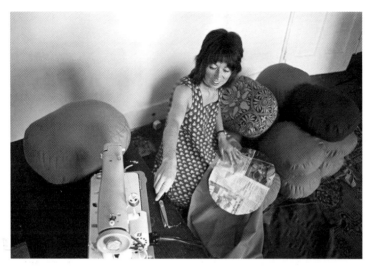

Making kusa cushions, 1976. (© Clear Vision)

Vajragita and Vajrapushpa sitting in front of the shrine after their ordinations, 1982. (© Clear Vision)

Sangharakshita (in robes rear view) seated as Vangisa (d.1981) talks from the podium. Order Convention, Vine Hall, 1978. (© the Sangkarakshita Archive)

Sangharakshita in robes at Padmaloka, 1977. (© the Sangharakshita Archive)

Sangharakshita (old clothes and sailor's hat with
sideburns) with Kevin Brooks (hat & pipe)
standing amongst sunflowers. 1970s.
(© the Sangharakshita Archive)

Sangharakshita & others (inc. Sagaramati & Nagabodhi)
at the meal table at Padmaloka, 1970s.
(© the Sangharakshita Archive)

Buddhafield, July 2009. (© Lokabandhu)

Laura & Gill in front of a shrine
at a North London parents' retreat.

Sangharakshita in the garden, Madhyamaloka, July 2009.
(© Alokavira/Timm Sonnenschein)

Bhante opening the Krakow Buddhist Centre, with Nityabandhu, September 2008. (© Roy Peters)

Women at the Order Convention, India 2009.
(© P.Rughani www.lotusfilms.co.uk)

Stupa in the warehouse at Windhorse Trading.
(© Jenny Henderson)

Silendrabhodhi meditating, India.
(© Dhammarati)

Story time, India. (© Dhammarati)

the USA, Australasia, and Europe. As one Order member wrote on his return home:

> Being at Bodh Gaya for the Order Convention was rather like finding myself in the midst of a long-held and deeply cherished dream. However, if you had asked me beforehand what the contents of the dream were, I doubt that I could have told you – only by being there did I discover that I had cherished this dream for a long time.... I can hardly believe how happy and fulfilled I felt being with several hundred brothers and sisters in the Order practising beneath the Bodhi Tree ... for the first time in my life, at the place where the Buddha gained Enlighten-ment all those years ago, I felt I could give full and wholehearted expression to my feelings of reverence and devotion with no inhibitions and no holding back.[107]

At the first convention, *Shabda,* a monthly newsletter to which any Order member could contribute, was launched. As time went on, Order convenors were appointed to oversee the organization of Order gatherings, to help chapters function effectively, and to mediate in cases of disharmony between Order members. The larger Order gatherings were often occasions where Sangharak-shita would give a talk or teaching, such as the 'FWBO System of Meditation' at the convention of 1978, or 'My Relation to the Order', given in April 1990.

❧

Another area in which care and resources have been invested over the years is in preparing people for ordination. This is because it is such a significant step for the individual involved. It is also seen as crucial for maintaining the spiritual integrity of the Order that those ordained really are practising the Buddhist path effectively and are able to join in fully with the life of the Order. Of course, anyone who is practising the Dharma is in 'training' all the time, but it has been in the preparation for ordination that the movement has concentrated most attention. While it may have been more elementary in the old days, gradually more carefully planned training programmes got under way. Their development in the women's wing has been described in the previous chapter; here we'll trace the evolution of ordination training for men.

In September 1981 the first three-month ordination retreat was held for men at Il Convento di Santa Croce, a former monastery of Augustinian Canons in Tuscany. The owner of the property staged operas there during the summer, but once the season was over, he was pleased to hire the place out in exchange for some rent and help with building work.

The men could prepare much better for ordination by having three months practising in ideal conditions, forming friendships, and spending more time with Sangharakshita – who initially attended all the retreats. Many also experienced a sense of 'going forth' more powerfully through making the journey to this unknown, yet beautiful place. They often returned home full of inspiration and, in the next five years, the Il Convento retreats became part of the life and soul of the movement.

During 1985, £150,000 had been raised for Sangharakshita's sixtieth birthday in order to buy him a secluded vihara. Searching for suitable land in the Sierra Altana Mountains of southern Spain, Subhuti and his companion followed a golden eagle, flying far above them. They ended up in a valley flanked by sheer limestone cliffs, which had formerly been terraced and planted out with almond trees, though pine trees and holm-oaks were gradually re-colonizing. It was stunningly beautiful, full of dramatic rock formations and, in the springtime, abounding in wild flowers: rock-roses, yellow-wort, cupidone, and wild orchids. The following year these 200 acres of land, with a small bungalow for Sangharakshita, were purchased; the place was then developed into an ordination retreat centre.

In 1987 the first ordination course was held at the new retreat centre, which Sangharakshita had named Guhyaloka – 'the secret realm'. Those attending the courses felt they'd travelled far from mundane life, and could practise in beautiful and ideal conditions. It was as if the tall mountain walls contained and protected them while they prepared for ordination.

The ordination process was changing back in the UK as well. In the late 1980s a new ordination team was formed at Padmaloka Retreat Centre, led by Subhuti, who quickly announced changes.

For most of the 1980s the training process at Padmaloka had culminated in month-long 'ordination selection retreats'. All those thought of as possible candidates for ordination that year were asked to attend. During the course of the month, some would get their invitation to Il Convento, others would be told they had more work to do and would hopefully be ordained the following year. The atmosphere on the retreats could be tense and strained, the potential ordinands hoping desperately they'd be selected, and feeling a sense of failure if they weren't.

This new system was to have much less emphasis on being 'selected' and more focus on helping everyone to Go for Refuge more effectively. That is what being 'ready for ordination' really meant: that you understood enough about yourself, about the Dharma, and about the context of the WBO that you could keep Going for Refuge effectively under reasonable circumstances.

The new team increased the number of training retreats and introduced new themes. Subhuti and others gave talks re-emphasizing key ideas and themes of the movement, such as 'Going for

Refuge', 'Spiritual Friendship', and 'What is the Order?'. They visited men's Order chapters around the UK, explaining how they wanted to work with local Order members in preparing men for ordination. The process had an energizing, invigorating effect on the movement. The number of men requesting ordination rose dramatically in the early and mid-1990s.

There were also changes designed to make the ordination process more accessible to those with family and work responsibilities. In its early days the FWBO had been predominantly a young movement, but this was changing. The new retreats had options for attending for a weekend, nine days, or the full two weeks, and allowed a more flexible approach to ordination training.

The most significant change of all was Sangharakshita's handing on of the responsibility for conferring ordinations. By this time he had ordained over 350 people, and it was becoming impossible to maintain a high degree of personal contact with all of them. He was also now over 60, and thinking of the continuation of the Order into the future. There were now Order members who'd been ordained for 15 years or more and who had the necessary experience and maturity to carry out ordinations.

The transition was handled carefully, as it was of such importance, both in terms of maintaining the spiritual integrity of the Order, and more symbolically – in that Sangharakshita was such a central figure. In 1985, Kamalashila, Subhuti and Suvajra conducted public ordinations for men in India on Sangharakshita's behalf. The following year, Padmasuri, Ratnasuri, and Srimala did the same for Indian women.

In January 1989, 130 people packed into the old shrine-room at Padmaloka at the end of a winter retreat. They witnessed six ordinations, the first in the West carried out on Sangharakshita's behalf. Subhuti and Suvajra had been the private preceptors; Subhuti now conducted the public ordination ceremony. It was significant for another reason as well.

Since the Il Convento retreats had got under way at the start of the 1980s, only two men had been ordained without attending the long retreat there, or at Guhyaloka. But the six men being ordained that day had either families or busy jobs and would have found it difficult, if not impossible, to attend a three or four-month retreat. While it was still thought preferable to attend those retreats if possible, more flexible arrangements were put in place that made ordination more realistic and accessible for a broader range of people.

Helping people prepare for ordination is a responsibility that Order members take very seriously and see as part and parcel of being in the Order. Since the late 1980s there has been a great increase in the number of private preceptors. More than 100 Order members have now taken on that role. More public preceptors have also been appointed. The process of trying to assess the effectiveness of someone else's Going for Refuge inevitably causes you to reflect on your own, so it can be spiritually revealing. When he was first coming to terms with that responsibility, Subhuti put it like this: '[Conferring ordinations] for me represents a far deeper level of responsibility than I have ever taken before. In witnessing someone else's Going for Refuge my own is called into question ...'[108] Again, the whole process was having a spiritually invigorating effect.

During the 1989 Guhyaloka ordination course, Subhuti and Suvajra ordained seven men, this time not under Sangharakshita's tutelage but under their own responsibility. It was, as Sangharakshita wrote, '... of the utmost significance for the future of the Order, and for me personally a source of the deepest satisfaction.'[109]

Twenty-one years after Sangharakshita had conducted the first ordinations into the Western Buddhist Order, these ordinations represented another crucial stage in transmitting the 'shared understanding' of Going for Refuge. He had ordained around

400 Order members by that time. The new preceptors were to ordain another 500 people during the 1990s. Within a decade, the majority of the Order had been ordained by Sangharakshita's disciples, rather than by the founder himself. A lineage had begun.

9
Handing On

Most new religious movements don't survive for very long. The odds of them lasting more than one hundred years are less than one in a thousand, according to some studies.[110] A particularly vulnerable time is when the founder hands on responsibility for the movement, or dies, and the next generation becomes fully responsible for the well-being of the community. There is very often disagreement about the correct interpretation of the founder's teachings, resulting in conflict and eventual schism. Or there is a loss of inspiration, and the movement slows to a standstill once the original teacher has gone.

Sangharakshita knew this, and had thought long and hard about the matter. He planned to hand over the responsibility for the FWBO carefully and gradually in his own lifetime. This would ensure there was a long – and hopefully stable – post-transition period during which he would still be around to act as a unifying figure, a guiding hand, and a guardian of the ideas and values enshrined in his movement.

In April 1990 he gave an important talk entitled 'My Relation to the Order'. He explained that while he would always occupy a unique position as the founder, as well as teacher and original preceptor to the Order and movement, he was now 'handing on'. The public preceptors had already begun to take responsibility for conducting ordinations. Then Sangharakshita resigned the position he had always held as president of all FWBO centres, and asked a number of senior Order members to step into that role too. The presidents were to act as 'spiritual friends' to the centres, helping to ensure they stayed true to the vision and principles of the FWBO.

Next, during the 1993 Order Convention, he called a meeting of the – still relatively new – public preceptors and presidents and told them he wanted to continue the process of passing on his responsibilities to them. He asked them to form a 'College of Public Preceptors' – to come and live together in a community, so that they could work closely together to protect and extend the work of the movement.

A big fundraising campaign was launched across the FWBO to buy property to house the new community, with office and meeting facilities. This was to be a gift to Sangharakshita on his seventy-fifth birthday. It would allow him not just to hand on, but also, after nearly thirty years of leading the movement, to move on into a new role and way of living.

The newly forming College wanted a property that was easily accessible from all over the UK and beyond. In 1994 Brackley Dene, a large Victorian house in suburban Birmingham, was purchased, and became Madhyamaloka ('the central realm'). Gradually the new community gathered: men in one building, women in another community down the road. It can't have been easy for some of them – having to pack up their possessions, move from where they had established lives, and then deal with the dynamics of a new community full of big personalities. As they unpacked, they may have wondered what on earth they were supposed to be doing. How did you form a 'Preceptors' College', and oversee a whole spiritual movement? How did you get a sense of what was going on out there in the big, wide world of the FWBO, let alone try to influence it? All their lives they'd done their best to serve Sangharakshita, and now he was asking them to take the lead in upholding and continuing his vision. They'd received from him something precious that they, in their turn, wanted to hand on faithfully. They felt it to be a weighty responsibility, but one that they wanted to honour to the best of their ability.

Two communities, secretarial support, and facilities for seminars and meetings were soon established. During the early 1990s and the setting up of the new ordination process for men, Subhuti emerged as a leading figure: able to grasp quickly and clearly the significance of Sangharakshita's teachings, forthright in propounding them, energetic and capable when it came to organizational matters. The mid to late 1990s were a similarly active and creative time for him. He wrote a biography of Sangharakshita (*Bringing Buddhism to the West*), and a book outlining and explaining his key ideas (*Sangharakshita: A New Voice in the Buddhist Tradition*).[111] He gave many talks too, for example, in 1995 speaking on the 'Hierarchy of Responsibility', and how Order members could grow and develop through taking spiritual and organizational responsibility in the newly emerging structures of the movement. The following year his talk on 'Unity and Diversity' was published, which sought to respond to the changes going on in the FWBO and show how those of different lifestyles could all contribute to the well-being of the sangha. Gradually, he and other members of the College were settling into their new roles, and it looked as if all was well.

❧

However, in the autumn of 1997, trouble was brewing. Down in London was the FWBO Communications Office, which was run by Vishvapani; he dealt with media enquiries and edited *Dharma Life*, the magazine he had launched a year before as the successor to *Golden Drum*. One day the phone rang and he found himself speaking to Madeleine Bunting, a journalist from the *Guardian*, one of the UK's main broadsheet newspapers. She said she wanted to write a lengthy piece on the FWBO, since it had recently celebrated its thirtieth birthday, but Vishvapani knew that she had written a disparaging piece on another Buddhist movement. Her article had attracted criticism in the UK Buddhist world for being one-sided and sensationalized. He suspected that it was now the FWBO's turn.

His suspicions were confirmed. It turned out that Bunting had been contacted by critics of the FWBO and given the case studies of three men. One was a former Order member who in the 1970s had had a close friendship and sexual relationship with Sangharakshita. In the late 1980s he had turned against Sangharakshita, maintaining that the relationship had been coercive and that the FWBO was a cult. He campaigned against the FWBO, attacking it in an interview on regional TV, and was eventually expelled from the Order. The second man had been involved in the Croydon Buddhist Centre and alleged that he had been pressured into homosexual sex with the centre chairman. The third case was that of a young man who had been involved in the Croydon Centre and who, three years after leaving the centre, had committed suicide. The implication was that these things had happened because the FWBO distorted Buddhist teachings and promoted homosexuality.

Vishvapani and others in the Communications Office tried to persuade the journalist that although things *had* gone badly wrong in a few instances in the past, the FWBO had tried to learn from those mistakes and that the overall allegations certainly weren't based on a correct interpretation of FWBO teaching. She interviewed numerous members of the Order about the issues that concerned her. As Vishvapani described it:

> Bunting's opinion changed as she researched her
> piece. The critics who had contacted her presented
> the FWBO as a sinister organization whose malevo-
> lence was testified by the bad experiences recounted
> in the press pack. But Bunting liked the people she
> met from the FWBO, and she expressed her respect
> for some of them. And yet … there were the testi-
> monies, the views that bothered her, the deadline
> approaching. … It is not that Bunting was unscru-
> pulous. But when she came to write her article I
> think the demands of telling a story left little room
> for the ambivalence that she expressed privately, nor
> the more rounded picture she had started to see.[112]

So it was that on 27 October 1997, the *Guardian* carried an
article entitled 'The Dark Side of Enlightenment' that went on
to tell of how '… the British-based cult is engulfed in allegations
that it manipulated vulnerable young men into becoming homosexual.'[113] Although the piece contained numerous qualifications
and riders, the overall impression was dark and disturbing.

The Communications Office submitted a complaint to the
Guardian, asserting that the article only gave one side of the argu-
ment, contained inaccuracies, and presented the issues in a sensationalized manner. Madeleine Bunting acknowledged some of
this. Some of the most lurid lines in the piece, such as the one
using the dreaded 'cult' word, had been the work of sub-editors;
she herself didn't think the FWBO was a cult. It seems that she was
perplexed by the FWBO; impressed by the genuineness and openness of those she'd met, yet troubled by the stories she'd heard.

She allowed Vishvapani to write a column putting the other
side of the story. The following week, Elizabeth Harris, a Buddhist
studies academic, wrote a column expressing an independent
view, yet one which was largely sympathetic to the FWBO.

There was also a forum organized by INFORM, an independent charity based at the London School of Economics and partly funded by the UK government, that provides information on new religious movements, and especially those that may be 'cults'.[114] The panel included Madeleine Bunting and Guhyapati, an Order member who worked with Vishvapani in the Communications Office. Academics from INFORM said they were impressed by the tone of the debate and how the FWBO had avoided a 'siege mentality'.[115]

The newspaper article seemed to have little effect on the numbers of new people coming along to FWBO centres. However, many of those already involved at centres, especially newer people who hadn't heard of those stories before, were disturbed and distressed by the article. Some did break off their involvement with the FWBO. Others felt that, on reflection, the FWBO being described in the newspaper bore no resemblance to the FWBO they were involved in. It didn't match their own experience of what it was like to attend Dharma classes, or go on retreat. In the Order, there was more debate. Some newer Order members had never heard these stories before, and were upset to read them. Others had been around for longer and had personal experience of the times described in the newspaper article. Even so, it was shocking to realize that was how some people viewed you, and to be portrayed that way by a major UK newspaper. What could the FWBO learn from the experience? There were numerous articles in *Shabda*, the Order's own newsletter, and also in *Dharma Life*, the FWBO magazine.

But the most virulent debate took place in Buddhist forums and discussion groups on the Internet. In May 1998 the 'FWBO Files', a long, detailed, anonymous document, was posted, making similar allegations to those that had appeared in the *Guardian* article.[116] It was becoming apparent that there was a small group of people waging a campaign to discredit the FWBO.

At around the same time, a complaint was made to the British government's then Education Minister, David Blunkett, about the work of Clear Vision (an FWBO charity based in Manchester) in the field of education. Clear Vision produces a wide range of videos and teaching materials for schools, and the accusation was that these were also based on a distorted view of Buddhism. It took almost a year for the Department of Education to complete their enquiry. In March 1999 Charles Clarke, Parliamentary Undersecretary for Education, wrote to the FWBO, rejecting the allegations. Clear Vision's work, which had been very well received throughout the education world, was vindicated. Other emails were sent anonymously to other government departments about the FWBO and NBO (the Network of Buddhist Organisations, of which the FWBO is a member). It became apparent that, though numerous, the complaints all issued from one person, the same person believed to be the author of the FWBO Files. This man was a British Buddhist who didn't believe that Sangharakshita had the authority to start a new Buddhist movement, and who had decided to anonymously attack the FWBO.

In August 1998 the FWBO Communications Office wrote a point-by-point rebuttal of the FWBO Files, detailing its catalogue of misquotes, quotes out of context, distortions, and sometimes plain and simple fabrications.[117] Later, in 2001, the webmaster of the website where the FWBO Files were posted (a young German man who'd fallen out with an Order member in Germany) wrote to a senior Order member, offering to take them off-line for $81,000. He wrote again with a similar offer in the autumn of 2004. Even if the original motive of the Files had been to promote debate about the FWBO, it had now become much more dubious. Those working in the Communications Office were not willing to respond to these demands for money; they knew that the webmaster could remove the FWBO Files from one website, but that the same material could easily be posted elsewhere.

Though the arguments raged on over the Internet, by the close of the 1990s it was a debate that was going round in circles, with nothing new revealed. Though the Internet criticism might not go away, the FWBO seemed to carry on and learn to live with it. There were people who were put off the FWBO after reading them; of these, some returned after a while. Overall, attendances at FWBO classes were steady, and there were even a number of new centres that opened during this period.

August 2000 was Sangharakshita's seventy-fifth birthday. A celebration was organized in the Great Hall of Aston University, Birmingham. Expectation filled the air, as it was known that he was going to make a special and significant announcement on that day. The occasion marked the final stage of his handing on. It must have been an extraordinary moment for him; he was later to reveal that every night in the preceding week, he had dreamed vividly of his own Buddhist teachers.

He explained that he was now passing on the 'Headship of the Order'. He wasn't burdening one person with too onerous a responsibility, but handing it on to the College of Public Preceptors collectively. However, he was going to appoint a chair of the College, who would serve for a five-year term, with the possibility of re-election by the other College members for a second term. Subhuti was to be the first chair of the College.

Subhuti then stood up and, on behalf of the College, accepted the responsibility that Sangharakshita was conferring on them.

> We accept it in gratitude to you, Bhante, for all you have done for us individually, as well as for so many others. We accept it, determined to stay faithful to you and to all you have taught us. We accept it with

reverence and love for you as our friend … may you
never be disappointed in us … [118]

Criticism had been survived, and now a highly significant transition had taken place. Amid the balloons, banners, and birthday
cake, it seemed that all was going to be well with the FWBO. But
an even more turbulent period in its history was yet to come.

10
Facing the Shadow

Subhuti and the other members of the College were now fully at the helm, and felt both more responsible and more free to take initiative in running the movement. The previous period had been an interregnum of sorts. Although Sangharakshita was stepping back and certainly less concerned with organizational issues, and the new generation had moved into position, they had not felt completely 'empowered'. But now that Sangharakshita had fully handed on, they were freer to act. They also thought it necessary to do so.

The movement was going through substantial changes. Some of these were due to its success, and with this success came a number of tensions and difficulties.

The 1990s had been the fastest period of growth in the Order to date. In 1994, it had 600 members; by 2003, there were more than 1,000. No longer was it a close, intimate group of Sangharakshita's personal disciples; it was now a large, worldwide community that he had founded in the (relatively) distant past. An increasing number of Order members had never even met him. No one could replace him. Although there were many impressive members of the Order, there was no one who seemed to live so fully in the realm of the Dharma as he.

Those in the FWBO in the old days had dreamt of the 'New Society' and worked hard to make the dream real. There had been a strong sense of participation in a common project, in a great, collective, creative effort. They'd achieved many of their dreams: in the UK especially, most major cities had an FWBO Buddhist centre; there were at least seven retreat centres, and plenty of communities and right livelihood enterprises. Yet this meant it could be harder to feel that sense of engagement in a common endeavour; the days of it being new and pioneering were over. There was even a tendency for the institutions to become rather centralized and conservative, which led to passivity on the ground.

Although the FWBO had achieved a measure of success in establishing itself in many countries around the world, this strained the systems and resources. As the movement became more spread out, more care was needed to maintain unity. There were now nearly 2000 people who had requested ordination worldwide, and consequently a growing need for ordination training processes to be established beyond the UK. All this stretched those senior Order members who were acting as presidents and public preceptors, and created tensions. Some Order members outside the UK felt that the FWBO was too 'UK-centric'; they were frustrated, and wanted more autonomy and control.

As the movement broadened, it was attracting people from a wider range of backgrounds and lifestyles. This success made only too obvious the increasing disparity between some of the old language and models of the FWBO and the current reality. For example, the idea of the 'New Society' had become associated with those living and working full-time in the institutions of the FWBO. There was still tension around 'lifestyle' (as described in Chapter 5).

Order members were growing in experience and spiritual maturity. Many had been practising for more than 15 years, and had been faithfully following the path of the FWBO. Increasingly they were having their own insights into the spiritual life, and wanted to teach more from their own experience, or explore other ways of practising, especially in the area of meditation. Again, there was much that was positive in this, but it started to raise the question of how the FWBO maintained and presented a coherent body of teaching.

In 2001 Subhuti formed a core working group around him, known as 'the Madhyamaloka meeting'. They decided to embrace all the changes going on, to work with them to try to free up new currents of energy in the movement. Their slogan, which encapsulated the spiritual and 'cultural' changes they felt were necessary, was: 'Deepen the Order, open up the Movement'.

To 'deepen the Order', there were talks and workshops designed to revitalize the Order chapter meetings, and a great number of chapters were invited to Madhyamaloka for a few days each, to work with Subhuti and others on making their chapters more spiritually dynamic. There were also plans for a 'Sangharakshita Library ', to preserve Sangharakshita's books, papers and effects, and, after his death, to act as a memorial. It would have around it a community of senior and experienced Order members who would run retreats and study seminars, and help to keep the spiritual vision shining bright and clear.

To 'open up the movement', there were changes to the Mitra system, which many people felt had become too complex and centralized. In August 2001 Subhuti gave a talk explaining how the Madhyamaloka meeting wanted to begin a process of decentralization of the College and structures of the movement, and there was an attempt to set up regional councils.

While some of these initiatives (such as the changes to the Mitra system) were welcomed in the Order, others (such as the library project and the planned regionalization) didn't get off the ground at this stage. What the College was able to achieve seemed limited. The Order was now too large, and the members of the College too few, and overworked at that. The Order works according to the principle of 'consensus' – important decisions are made once all Order members either agree with the decision, or are willing to align themselves with it. But how did you seek, and measure, consensus on major issues when the whole Order needed to be involved? Some people commented that true cultural change doesn't come from above. The Order had gone past the phase when it could be influenced in a simple way, through talks, seminars, and exhortation. Though sincerely motivated, the change was too much driven from the centre. Subhuti was much admired, and a brilliant leader and organizer, but the times seemed to call for leaders who were able to work more organically and consensually. Though Subhuti tried to adapt his style, it didn't come naturally to him.

While the other College members were liked and respected too, it was obvious that not all of them were suited to, or even interested in, this kind of organizational responsibility. Some of them had been working hard at the forefront of the movement for many years, and felt the need for personal change. A number of the original College members moved on.

Sangharakshita was also struggling. He had been active and vigorous well into his seventies, but now he seemed to slide quickly into old age. His eyesight deteriorated, due to macular degeneration, which he bore with remarkable equanimity. Then he started suffering from severe insomnia, and, with that, extreme exhaustion, which he found terribly distressing. It was shocking for his close disciples to see him like this, and he confided to a friend that while he had felt prepared for death, he hadn't felt prepared for old age. In a matter of months, he had become a fragile old man. He asked not to be bothered by anything at all. To help cope with his insomnia, he didn't want to hear of news or developments in the movement; he just wanted to be left undisturbed.

Those left at Madhyamaloka looked after Sangharakshita as best they could, and wondered what to do with the movement. The issues with which they were trying to grapple were knotty and intertwined, and they felt tangled and tied down by them. Somehow, it wasn't working. Something was holding the Order back.

Then a letter was written which changed everything.

The Order-only publication *Shabda* offers a place for any member of the WBO to write about aspects of their life and practice. Each month the letters received are collated, printed, and distributed throughout the Order; thus the newsletter is one of its main mediums for discussion and communication.

In January 2003 an Order member named Yashomitra submitted his report to *Shabda*. It contained his account of his sexual relationship with Sangharakshita in the early 1980s. At the time, Yashomitra was only 18; Sangharakshita was nearly 40 years older than him, and was his preceptor and teacher. The relationship had gone on for about six months and then Sangharakshita had ended it. In retrospect, Yashomitra regretted the relationship and felt it had been harmful to him. How could Sangharakshita have been so unaware of how impressionable Yashomitra would have been, and of how likely it was that he would get hurt? Yashomitra wanted to tell the Order about this. He thought that there were other men struggling with these issues, and that the Order collectively had still not faced up to the shadows of the past.

The compiler of *Shabda* asked the Madhyamaloka meeting for advice. Should he print a letter that was so personal and so critical of someone, especially when that someone was the founder of the Order?

It wasn't until the following month that all the members of the meeting were able to gather together to discuss it. They knew the contents of the letter were explosive. What were they to do? If they printed the letter, Sangharakshita might feel betrayed. They even worried that, in his fragile state, the shock and distress might kill him. They also felt sure, however, that for its own health and integrity, the Order had to be open and honest.

When the FWBO Files had been posted on the Internet, the official response written by the FWBO Communications Office had played down and avoided the issue of Sangharakshita's sex life. This was at the request of leading Order members in India, where homosexuality is still taboo. They were concerned that revelations that Sangharakshita was homosexual would not just upset people, but even risk social unrest and violence in the highly charged world of Ambedkarite politics. This had, however, left those Order members in the Communications Office – and others in the West – in an uncomfortable situation where they couldn't be open about an issue they knew concerned many people. Now, knowing that the news had gone public in India, they were willing to compromise no longer.

The Madhyamaloka meeting decided to publish. In March 2003 Yashomitra's letter was printed in *Shabda* with the following preface by Subhuti:

> Yashomitra writes with honesty and objectivity and raises issues that, in our view, do need to be aired in the Order and movement, whether or not one agrees with everything that he says. Indeed I am glad that Yashomitra has written the article and am pleased that another piece of our collective history is being opened to us all.[119]

Previous criticism had come from outside the movement, but Yashomitra was well known and well liked. However, whereas the *Guardian* article had been sensationalist, and the FWBO Files had been vindictive, Yashomitra was quietly reasonable. His letter had an air of authenticity which was impossible to ignore.

Its publication sparked a process of questioning, debate, and soul-searching that blazed away for months. For some time, *Shabda* was full of opinions and reflections, stories and reminiscences, including those of some of the men who had been sexually involved with Sangharakshita, or with other senior Order members, or women who had experienced disapproval and hostility when they had decided to have families, or those who had been involved in the Croydon Buddhist Centre. Some of these stories were, with the authors' permission, reprinted in a booklet that was made available to Mitras and others in the FWBO, so that they could be informed of the issues. There was shock and disbelief, followed by anger and then sadness. There were expressions of loyalty, feelings of betrayal. There was also relief that it had all finally come out into the open.

Sangharakshita was ill and didn't even know what was going on, the College were under increasing strain of work, and several of them had moved away. Who was going to hold things together through the crisis? The College realized they just needed to get out of the way and allow the Order to debate the issues as it wanted. Subhuti wrote another letter in the May 2003 edition of *Shabda*, encouraging complete honesty and freedom of comment about the past. That summer, the Order Convention was largely based around two 'forums' where issues were talked about openly.

The forums were carefully and skilfully facilitated by Dhammadinna and Nagabodhi. They encouraged the five hundred or so Order members assembled there not to try to interpret, explain, or criticize other people's experience, or even to assume that they knew what that experience was. They explained that the aim was just to listen to people's stories, or, if you spoke, to do so from your own experience, rather than theories or opinions about the FWBO's past. The atmosphere was electric and edgy. 'Can't we just get on with it?' someone shouted out. 'Yes, we'll start soon', said Nagabodhi, 'but first I'd just like to sing you a song.' Everyone burst into laughter, some tension released, and then they got on with it. For several hours, Order members stood up and told their tales of those early days. As described by one Order member who was sitting listening:

> Although much of what was being talked about was outside my direct personal experience, I remember beginning to weep, then noticing how many others were too, men and women, as if a collective gestalt session were going on. It was not a debate attempting a resolution, which was impossible ... It felt like a coming of age too ... [120]

❧

The questioning and discussion provoked by Yashomitra's letter raged round three interrelated issues. First, there was Sangharakshita and sex. Quite a number of young men, all aged 18 or over, but still much younger than Sangharakshita, had had sexual relationships with him in the early days. Many had been quite happy about this, but, for at least a few, it had become problematic. Had he been unethical, not taking their situation and feelings into account? If so, did this undermine his credibility as a Buddhist teacher?

Secondly, it raised wider questions about sex, the FWBO, and the 'experimental' culture that had been prevalent in its early days.

Thirdly, the article also acted as a catalyst, setting off a chain reaction of other issues. People were not just talking about Sangharakshita's sex life, but assessing their own relationship to the FWBO over a whole range of topics. It reignited various controversies from the past: the pain and unhappiness of those who'd felt excluded and disapproved of because they'd not been living the 'full FWBO lifestyle'; the old tensions between the men's and the women's wings; further disagreement with Sangharakshita's views on the spiritual aptitude of men and women; and issues around hierarchy and authority.

It is impossible to do justice to all the views that were expressed, but once the flames died down and the dust began to settle, most people probably felt something along the following lines ...

❧

They still felt deeply grateful to Sangharakshita for having started the FWBO and giving them the Dharma. From what they saw of how he behaved in other areas of his life, they didn't believe he had deliberately manipulated his lovers. Yet they could see that he seriously underestimated the way people were in awe of him, and therefore might be swept along. He hadn't realized how difficult it might be for some of those young men to know what they really wanted, or to be able to say 'no'.

Sangharakshita did not conduct his relationships in secret. At the time, they were widely known about. But when the allegations were made, he refused to discuss them publicly and did not express any regret. Order members were pained by what they experienced as a barrier in communication. They realized that Sangharakshita was a private man and that most people wouldn't want to talk about their sex life in public. They understood that this might be especially true for someone of Sangharakshita's generation; he was now in his late seventies. Equally, they sympathized with his fear that anything he said would be misunderstood, or possibly misinterpreted on the Internet. Yet they still wished that he had said something, perhaps simply stating that he hadn't intended to harm anyone, and that he was sorry if that had happened.

During the period of his life in which he was sexually active (he was celibate in the late 1960s and became so again in the late 1980s), he sometimes still wore the orange robes of a Theravadin monk, especially on ceremonial occasions and in India, even though Theravadin monks are celibate. Sangharakshita had explained this by saying that he was trying to establish a new kind of ordination that was neither monastic nor lay, and that he strongly experienced himself as a kind of hybrid between the two. It was hard for people to imagine what it was like for him pioneering Buddhism in the West, seeking to act as a transitional figure between old traditions and new. Yet, in hindsight, most felt the wearing of these particular robes while being sexually active to be a mistake that had caused inevitable confusion.

❧

The counterculture of the late 1960s and early 1970s was also the era of sexual liberation. Many of the young people coming into the FWBO were influenced by ideas of free love and sexual experimentation. As their Buddhist practice started to go deeper, however, many of them became increasingly aware of the time and energy they were investing in sex, and felt it was a distraction from practice. They were also seeing how strongly they were influenced by the Western 'romantic ideal' – an unconscious expectation of finding the one person with whom to experience perfect love and sexual intimacy. This could lead to unhealthy, over-attached relationships. A robust critique of this 'neurotic relationship' emerged within the FWBO.

Here were men and women, mostly in their twenties and thirties, trying to apply Buddhism within the arena of sex and relationships. They were attempting to work out the implications of the Dharma in a particular sphere of their lives, for a new time and cultural context. It didn't seem possible or appropriate simply to copy the Asian monastic model, but they didn't want to go along with their Western cultural conditioning either.[121]

Partly in order to enable men and women to live more freely of romantic or sexual attachment, single-sex communities and retreats began to develop. By the mid-80s, the single-sex idea was a very strong and integral part of FWBO culture. People related to this in different ways, as described by Dhammadinna:

> For me, moving to a single-sex lifestyle went along with giving up sex. For others it meant engaging in same-sex sex. Some people did this for a while, perhaps realizing they were more bisexual than they thought, while others discovered their true orientation was towards their own gender. Other people remained heterosexual, and still others became celibate. We were trying to break taboos, perhaps derived from Christian and social attitudes to sex, which sometimes resulted in irrational guilt. Some people began to speculate that homosexuality might be in some way more "spiritual" than heterosexuality, because it was less likely to lead to domesticity and settling down. We also discussed whether spiritual friendship and sexual involvement went together.[122]

But later, as more people with families got involved in the FWBO, such a strong advocacy of the single-sex idea could appear discouraging to them. For example, there was an often-used phrase about 'keeping your sexual relationship at the edge of your mandala'.[123] For a young person trying to practise the Dharma more intensively, and wanting to keep their romantic and sexual involvement balanced and not all-encompassing, the phrase could be helpful. But to someone practising in a family context, responsible for a partner and family, it seemed strange and inappropriate. So did some of the FWBO rhetoric about the 'neurotic couple' – two people who were emotionally over-dependent on each other – being 'the enemy of the spiritual community'.[124] Its tone could come across as crude, confrontational, and off-putting to those who were living with partners or families.

Times were changing in other ways too. The 1980s saw the advent of the AIDS tragedy, and of Clause 28 in the UK.[125] There was growing alarm about sexual abuse, and discussion of political correctness and gender politics. All these reflected – and helped create – very different attitudes to sex and sexuality than had prevailed in the 1960s. As Dhammadinna reflected:

> ... some of the things we did in the past have given rise to controversy. Perhaps it is time to take stock; to look back on those early experiments, and consider what was learned and what has been left behind. This means understanding the attitudes and activities of previous decades in the context of their time. We should be aware of the tendency to see the past through the eyes of the present. ...[126]

People were now taking stock in the area of sex and spiritual friendship. Could sex help people break through into deeper friendship and communication, or were sex and spiritual friendship best kept apart?

Sangharakshita had spoken about men often having a fear of homosexuality and a fear of physical contact with other men, and this fear being a barrier to deeper friendship. But, as he said in an interview in the late 1980s: 'This is not necessarily to say that they should have sexual contact with men ...'[127] By this time, he had also returned to the practice of celibacy, having come to the conclusion that,

> sex didn't really play much of a part in human communication ... it didn't result in a permanent breakthrough: it only gave one a certain opportunity, which one then had to develop. Sometimes the breakthrough came to an end and things were as they were before ...[128]

More widely in the FWBO, many people were coming to the same conclusion: while sex between friends didn't preclude genuine spiritual friendship, it didn't necessarily or generally lead to a deepening of friendship either.[129]

A number of other new Buddhist sanghas, especially in the USA, had gone through periods of intense controversy and debate about sex between 'teachers' and 'students'. Like them, the FWBO was learning that sex in the sangha could be dangerous. If one party was older or more spiritually experienced than the other, naive faith in the former as a teacher, desire for their approval, and abdication of personal responsibility could easily occur. Powerful emotions could be released as people got involved in the spiritual life. So those who were liable to be seen as 'teachers' or in positions of 'authority' needed to be very careful.

Certainly, from the mid-1990s onwards, most people in the FWBO would probably advise caution in the area of sex and spiritual friendship. There were calls for a 'code of conduct', and many FWBO centres did have an agreement that teachers and team members would not proposition anyone at meditation and Buddhism classes. Beyond this, it seemed difficult to make 'rules', as how would you enforce them? The area needed to be negotiated through trust and discussion, not regulations. And, as Dhammadinna noted:

> In a Buddhist movement of the size and diversity of the FWBO – which is active in cultures as different as the modern US, India, and South America – any attempt to dictate norms of behaviour could become enormously complex.[130]

❧

The reaction to Yashomitra's letter was also about Order members – individually and collectively – coming into a more healthy relationship with their teacher. In the early days, people had been in awe of Sangharakshita. He was in his forties, while most of them were in their twenties. They were just discovering the Dharma, while he had been practising for more than twenty years, and was confident and inspired. Many people assumed he was Enlightened, though he never made any such claim. As one Order member from that time experienced it: 'The adulation and projection were massive. People breathed in and spoke Bhante's every word, and spoke no other; they pored over every syllable, every remark, every action.'[131]

Sometimes, Sangharakshita tried to play down the adulation. In the talk 'My Relation to the Order', given in 1990, he asked to be thought of simply as a spiritual friend; perhaps even just a friend. He didn't want to be considered a 'guru'. He believed that term created unhealthy expectations in the eyes of the followers, and might tempt the teacher into inflated views too. Even back then, he was pointing out to his followers that, obviously and inevitably, he had limitations:

It is partly because I am a rather complex person that I am a mystery to myself ... not so much of a mystery to myself as to cherish many illusions about myself. One of the illusions which I do *not* cherish is that I was the most suitable person to be the founder of a new Buddhist movement. ... I possessed so few of the necessary qualifications; I laboured under so many disadvantages. ... I cannot but feel that the coming into existence of the Western Buddhist Order was little short of a miracle. ... That one is a person at all means that one has certain limitations ... imposed by the fact that one is of a particular temperament and experiences life in a particular kind of way. One can hardly be of all temperaments and experience life in every kind of way ... my own personal limitations should not be the limitations of the Order. The Order should not simply be Sangharakshita writ large. ... The Order should be a rich and many-splendoured thing, with all kinds of facets.[132]

Now, 13 years after Sangharakshita gave this talk, the Order was taking its message on more fully; they were coming to a much more mature and nuanced view of their teacher. It was as if a massive collective projection was being withdrawn from Sangharakshita. One can only imagine what this was like for him.

As Subhuti wrote in *Shabda* in 2003:

One could even see spiritual life as a process of maturing relationships with spiritual teachers ... If one's teacher is such a remarkable man as Bhante, that is not going to be an easy process. I hope we can be tolerant of ourselves and of others as we go through it. And I would like to suggest we be tolerant of teachers as they go through it too.[133]

In November 2004, a good 18 months after Yashomitra's letter, Subhuti gave two talks at Padmaloka.[134] To have one of Sangharakshita's closest and most senior disciples speaking about the current situation was highly significant and helpful.

Subhuti spoke of how – like all those who had been around in the early days – he'd always known Sangharakshita had been sexually active; they hadn't quite understood it, but they assumed he knew what he was doing. Now Yashomitra's letter had forced Subhuti to confront the issues more squarely. Like many in the Order, he had been through a struggle, reassessing his relationship with his teacher. Had Sangharakshita been horribly misunderstood and misrepresented, and was he really the perfect teacher they had always thought they'd had? Or was the picture of Sangharakshita depicted on the Internet true? Eventually, Subhuti had one of those realizations where it suddenly became obvious. He was never going to be able to tidy all the facts about this complex man either into a box labelled 'good', or another box labelled 'bad'. He was going to have to live with the paradox, accept the contradiction. Sangharakshita was an astonishing figure: an intellectual giant, a kind and skilful teacher, and full of genuine insights into the spiritual life. He was also a human being.

❧

All communities experience mistakes and messy conflicts; it is part of life. What marks out a healthy community is an ability to face and deal with that. The Order and FWBO were no exception. The extraordinary burst of creativity which had established a new Buddhist movement was also, sometimes, accompanied by a youthful arrogance that thought it had all the answers, or a dogmatic application of the teachings, or frictions arising out of discomfort with different styles and opinions.

At the same time, the community that emerged out of all this history does have a basic honesty and integrity, and a solid commitment to one another and to the Dharma. Although, sadly, some people, including Yashomitra, resigned from the Order between 2003 and 2005, the vast majority stayed. It is obviously not possible to generalize about those 1,500 people and their individual reasons for leaving or staying. However, while a community might easily have imploded in such a crisis, the Order and the movement were largely able to face the shadow and start to move on.

August 2005 was the month both of the biennial International Order Convention and of Sangharakshita's eightieth birthday. His health had improved dramatically, he was making public appearances again, and he was going to be at the convention. As had happened on many previous conventions, a birthday party was organized, with Order members reading poems, and performing music and comedy sketches. Sangharakshita sat in the front row, chortling away. It was just like the old days. Only it wasn't; it was more relaxed and real.

At the end, there was applause and Sangharakshita walked slowly and quietly out into the night air. One Order member immediately stepped forward and said how relieved he'd felt that they'd collectively been able to convey their indebtedness to their teacher. Many others felt the same sense of relief. For them, the break in communication had been healed, a connection reaffirmed, and gratitude re-expressed.

11

An Ever-Widening Circle

Of course, a resolution isn't as neat and tidy as that. People were processing the issues at their own pace, and coming to a whole spectrum of conclusions. By 2005, however, a tangible sense of confidence was returning.

During this time, the Preceptors' College had been pressing ahead with organizational restructuring, trying to respond to the pressures described at the beginning of the previous chapter. It may seem strange that such important changes were being made in the midst of a crisis. But the strain of their workload was such that they felt reorganization was urgent and vital. Nor were the changes they were proposing unconnected to the issues running their course through the Order.

During 2003 there was consultation in the Order on the restructuring of the Preceptors' College. Most people were broadly happy with what was proposed, and so it went ahead the following year. The changes were essentially a clarification of where authority and responsibility lay. They were summed up in the phrases, 'the movement runs the movement, the Order runs the Order, and the College runs the College'.

The Preceptors' College was no longer going to try to oversee the whole FWBO. Instead, those directly involved in running FWBO centres would move into that role, particularly the European FWBO Chairs Assembly, a twice-yearly meeting of chairs of FWBO projects in Europe. Since 2006 it has employed a small team of people (the FWBO Development Team) to help them with this work.

Nor was the College going to oversee the Order, which was to be responsible for its own spiritual vitality and harmony, and which needed to develop its own structures and decision making procedures.

The College remained responsible for maintaining the spiritual integrity of the Order through ensuring that those ordained were effectively Going for Refuge, and had an adequate training in the Dharma and in the ethos of the Order. Because of the special significance of that role, and because many of the members of the College are senior and experienced members of the Order, they have a particular responsibility for protecting and furthering Sangharakshita's vision and his emphases and insights into the Dharma.

There were new, more flexible working arrangements for the public preceptors, and more public preceptors were appointed. Lastly, in 2005, his five-year term being completed, Subhuti decided not to stand for re-election as chair of the College. Dhammarati became the new chair. Previously the chair of the London Buddhist Centre, he has more recently been working as the FWBO's liaison officer, building and maintaining links with other Buddhist sanghas.

❧

Despite all the difficulties, the FWBO held together. Surprisingly, given the sense of crisis, the movement carried on expanding during this period. The Order grew faster than ever, with one third of the Order being ordained in the five years since the publication of Yashomitra's letter. There was questioning of the past, people were taking stock, but they were also, quietly, getting on with their practice.

New centres or groups have started in places like Blackburn, Deal, and Worcester in Britain, as well as in Barcelona, Krakow, Sao Paulo and other locations beyond the UK. Existing centres steadily developed. For example, the London Buddhist Centre undertook its biggest building project since being established in 1979. They marked their thirtieth anniversary in 2008 by opening 'Breathing Space' – a new venue for more 'secular' activities, such as courses teaching mindfulness techniques to help those suffering from depression. Breathworks (discussed in Chapter 5) was born in 2003 and continues to grow rapidly. There has also been discussion of how to communicate the Dharma to young people. Clear Vision, with their experience in producing educational resources on Buddhism, plans to provide free online Dharma aimed at young people. Furthermore, 2009 saw younger people involved at FWBO centres in the UK beginning to network and talk about their experience of practising in the FWBO.

In the 1990s, a new project named 'Buddhafield' had started running cafés and teaching meditation at festivals in the UK. They also ran camping retreats with a strong emphasis on ritual and ecological awareness, and founded the 'Buddhafield Festival' – an annual gathering of people from the FWBO and many other ecological, spiritual, and alternative groups. By 2005 the festival was attracting over 2,000 people. Inspired by the original Buddhafield project, which is based in the southwest of England, people from other regions started running camping retreats, giving rise to 'Buddhafield East' and 'Buddhafield North'.

The FWBO has responded to the rise of the Internet, perhaps most impressively with the old Dharmachakra Tapes evolving into Free Buddhist Audio, a website where hundreds of talks by Sangharakshita and other Order members are available for free.[135] On current trends, one million talks will have been downloaded in the website's first five years. The site also hosts the study material for the new training course for Mitras that was launched in 2009.[136] Wildmind is another website that teaches meditation and Buddhism online.[137]

In recent years, Sangharakshita's health has improved and he has become more publicly active again. He has travelled to many centres in Europe, giving talks and question-and-answer sessions. He continues to live quietly at Madhyamaloka in Birmingham, receiving a steady stream of visitors and replying to a constant flow of letters. In 2009, USA-based Wisdom Publications published *The Essential Sangharakshita*, a 760-page anthology of a lifetime's writing.[138] That one of the world's major Buddhist publishers produced such a large volume of his writings was a remarkable tribute to his importance as a translator of the Dharma for the West.

❧

Strengths of the FWBO

What is the key to the success of the FWBO? What are the particular strengths that allowed it to thrive, mature, and stay united – even during challenging times?

1) Clear and accessible Dharma teaching

Sangharakshita has been a skilled teacher, clearly explaining the essential vision of the Dharma and ways of applying it to our lives. His teaching draws on the breadth of the Buddhist tradition, pointing out the underlying unifying principles. He has made use of Western concepts and culture, but has done so with great care and thoughtfulness, remaining faithful to the spirit of the Dharma.

He has also taught others how to teach. The FWBO has become well known for a high standard of Dharma and meditation teaching, for making the Dharma accessible to newcomers, and for a substantial degree of Dharma knowledge in those who've been ordained (achieved largely through the Mitra training course and ordination training).

2) Sangha and friendship

The FWBO has also succeeded because of its emphasis on sangha and friendship, on authenticity and communication, and on the support that is gained from these. Many people have practised, lived, worked, and been on retreat together, and this has created lifelong bonds of friendship which hold the sangha together. There has been an emphasis on creating contexts – such as residential communities or right livelihood projects – which can help create a more 'intensive' interaction between members of the sangha. In the Order, there are well-developed forums and channels for meeting and communicating, and these have stood it in good stead. The emphasis on open communication often enables difficulties to be faced and talked about, and harmony restored.

Valuing the practice of friendship and trying to be concerned for other people also grounds the spiritual life in the human and everyday, and guards against the danger of it becoming rather self-preoccupied and 'other-worldly'.

3) Unity and diversity

From New York to Nagpur, from Johannesburg to Oslo, from Mexico City to Melbourne, the approach of the FWBO has allowed an increasingly diverse group of people from different classes and cultures to get involved in Buddhist practice. They may come from many different walks of life, but they tread the same path of the Dharma.

The Order has grown larger, more diverse, and more spread out geographically. Yet, if two Order members from opposite sides of the world meet for the first time, there will still be a basic trust, openness, and recognition of what they hold in common. They will feel part of the same community. That is a remarkable testimony to the unity and harmony of the Order.

4) Taking the Dharma out into the world

The FWBO has always stressed the importance of spreading the Dharma, and of finding ways to reapply the essential principles in a new time and situation. What light can the Dharma shed on work and economics, families and relationships, arts and education, or social and environmental problems? This outward-going, innovative, exploratory emphasis has been a great strength of the FWBO. Many people in the FWBO are engaged in the challenges of bringing the Dharma to new cultures, and exploring the implications of Buddhism for Western society. They are trying to create a *modern* Buddhism. Often people coming into the FWBO feel they would not have connected with traditional Buddhism, and feel grateful that the FWBO gave them the Dharma in a form relevant to today.

❧

In the early days, all this was innovative and revolutionary. There's a danger that now the FWBO (and other Dharma groups in the West) are established, it can seem obvious and ordinary, and we may start to take it for granted. If, in the early days of the FWBO, the teaching could be expressed rather zealously, then perhaps a danger of the future – as everything becomes more established – is that the teaching is applied in a weakened and diluted form, and loses its vitality. The FWBO will need to maintain a sense of adventure, keep an exploratory edge. It will need to keep looking outwards, trying to communicate with new people, and apply the Dharma to new situations.

It's important to remember just how liberating it can be for someone to discover a spiritual path that speaks to them, or to experience new dimensions of awareness and emotional expansion through meditation, or to find a community in which their deepest values are encouraged, respected, and mirrored back.

❧

On the day in November 1997 that the *Guardian* newspaper article was published, Sanghadeva, a loyal and long-standing Order member, had phoned the newspaper's offices, and asked to be put through to the journalist, Madeleine Bunting. He told her that he disagreed with 95% of what she'd said in her article, but he wanted to thank her for writing it. It would help the FWBO face up to the difficulties of the past, and reflect more deeply on its history.

He thought the critics had got much of it wrong. But neither did the FWBO get it all right. It had to develop a deeper maturity, albeit painfully. Although confidence gradually returned, it was a confidence that was quieter, more grounded in people's own individual experience, and not just the theory.

So what is the moral of the story? What is this more mature understanding of the spiritual life? Here is an attempt to summarize a few of the lessons the FWBO has learned.[139] It is a personal view, rather than an 'official account'. Probably, many other Western sanghas would draw up a similar list. In writing this,

I'm not claiming that people in the FWBO are, individually or collectively, perfectly wise! It is an ongoing process. Yet my list *is* intended to be a celebration of work well done, of a hard-won maturity, of a 'collective wisdom' that has been gained.

Lessons Learned

1) We go for refuge with our imperfections

All of us bring weaknesses, mixed motives, blind spots, and biases into our involvement with a sangha and the spiritual life. This means that we will, inevitably, make mistakes. Disputes and disagreements, difficult dynamics, and failed relationships are bound to occur. They *will* happen; the issue is how we respond to them.

The Buddha taught that everything in the world is characterized by 'unsatisfactoriness' because of our desire for things to be a certain way . The causes and conditions that they depend on are so complex and ever-changing that things will never turn out *exactly* how we want. What we can sometimes forget is that this teaching is true of spiritual communities as well.

If we've come along to the spiritual life naively expecting it to be perfect, then it can easily turn sour. We're hurt, and we want to avoid that pain, so we push away from the sangha. We blame others; we especially blame 'institutions'. We fantasize to ourselves that it would have been all right if only *this* person hadn't got involved, or *that* person had acted in a different way. Disillusionment hardens into disgruntlement. Cynics are often disgruntled idealists.

These failures *are* painful and humiliating. It may be that we *were* treated badly by others. We need to take all this seriously, but not too personally. We see the disillusioning experience as an opportunity to go beyond our limitations, and develop more patience and loving-kindness. We learn how to forgive failure – both in ourselves and in others.

According to the psychologist James Hillman, 'initiation into a new consciousness of reality comes through betrayal'.[140] His sometimes provocative statements warn against expecting relationships to be completely safe and fulfilling. People *will* let us down; this is not only inevitable, it is also how we grow up.

If you read the Pali canon – the earliest surviving record of the Buddha's life and teaching – you will find numerous stories about the sangha he founded. In many of them the Buddha has to intervene in petty quarrels, clear up monks' confusions about the teachings, and settle arguments about the correct way to conduct rituals. It is oddly reassuring to know that, even though those monks had the Buddha living with them, it was not all sweetness and light.

The FWBO has developed a deeper understanding of how – to paraphrase Samuel Beckett – the spiritual life is a process of failing, trying again, failing better. In the Order, particularly, there is growing skill and experience in how to mediate when things go wrong.

2) We don't know the consequences of our actions

The Buddhist teaching of karma states that an ethically skilful action will bring an element of happiness and satisfaction, an ethically unskilful action will lead to suffering. In real life situations, however, many more complex conditions are at play. Although we try to act with a skilful *intention*, we can't predict the exact *outcome*. There are often unforeseen consequences.

There's a seeming paradox here: we need to act boldly and ambitiously while at the same time holding onto our ideas provisionally . We remain sensitive to the fact that we don't know the full consequences of our actions. We are prepared to review and change course. A community that is applying ancient principles to a new situation has, by necessity, to experiment and innovate – and to be especially willing to learn and adapt too.

The 1960s and early 1970s were revolutionary times and it was easy to get intoxicated, to think that we were the ones who were going to put the world to rights, and show the old guard how it should be done. But, sooner or later, the world teaches us humility.

In its early days, the FWBO's discourse could be rather harsh and ringing, and relations with other Buddhist groups were sometimes tense and distrustful. The situation is much better these days. The FWBO is an active and valued participant in inter-Buddhist bodies such as the UK Network of Buddhist Organisations, or the European Buddhist Union. Many other Western sanghas are curious about the FWBO and admiring of its success. The FWBO has learned to be confident and proud of the distinctive contribution it makes, but also increasingly modest, unpretentious, and willing to learn from others.

3) Remember the spirit behind the practice

Sometimes we don't like this apparent ambiguity; we prefer to have clear-cut, certain answers. Literalism is the tendency to grasp tightly the words with which a truth or teaching is expressed, so that the underlying meaning is squeezed out. We grab hold of the letter of the law, and miss the spirit in which the teaching was given. We can do this with *any* teaching or practice.

Perhaps this is particularly a danger when we lack experience. Not having a deep and sustained personal experience of the practice, we rely on the 'theory' – on the letter of the law. In the early days of the FWBO it was, perhaps, not surprising that practices such as single-sex could become rigid and dogmatic. These days, more people have had the theory *and* tried the practice. Their approach is more human and more kind.

4) Beware of identifying the spiritual life with a particular lifestyle or teaching

Despite the principle of 'commitment primary, lifestyle secondary', a particular lifestyle did become normative in the early FWBO. It did work for many people, and there was an objective need to build a new movement, which helped make it legitimate to emphasize and promote that lifestyle. Yet it was done in a way that put off those for whom it didn't work. Over time, people in the FWBO have got better at not identifying the spiritual life with a particular lifestyle, and at valuing the contribution that people of different lifestyles can make.

We don't need to compare ourselves to those leading a different lifestyle, or doing a different practice, in a way that makes us either despondent or complacent. We can recognize that our spiritual life will go through many phases. We will need to practise in different ways at different times. Sometimes we may go on more retreats, sometimes go out to teach others. Sometimes our meditation needs to be simple and unembellished, and other times we respond to elaborate and colourful rituals. All these ways of practising are part of the process, another phase on the path. All will have their own lessons to teach you. We can value where we're at, and the teachings we've got; we don't need to look down on the 'basic practices' that have got us to where we are, nor be overawed by the idea of 'advanced practices' that lie ahead.

5) Have a patient faith in the Dharma

Aiming for Enlightenment *does* involve a radical reorientation of our lives, becoming more concerned with what we can *give* to life, rather than what we *get* from it. Yet profound, earth-shattering visions and transformations do not occur every day. Mostly, the spiritual life trundles along fairly ordinarily. We learn to 'trust the process'. What is important is learning to live more ethically and kindly. We don't need to be over-concerned with having special 'experiences' in meditation, although if they do occur, we can hopefully feel free to talk with appropriate friends about them.

We often underestimate the progress we've made, because it manifests in 'ordinary' and hard-to-measure ways – being less anxious here, more kind to that person, more able to speak our mind there. Friends may notice how we change more than we do. The spiritual life is both very ordinary and utterly amazing – and often at the same time.

6) Don't compartmentalize the spiritual life

'Unless your work is your meditation, your meditation is not meditation', Sangharakshita once said.[141] Our practice doesn't just happen in the shrine-room, but has to be integrated into the rest of our life – into our work and also our friendships and relation-ships of all kinds. We're trying to see the Dharma in the everyday, to sense the possibility of bringing more awareness and loving-kindness to every moment.

Seeing Going for Refuge as a moment-by-moment process has been one of the strengths of the FWBO approach. And yet, because of the early emphasis on a particular, single-sex lifestyle, areas of life were left out. For example, Order members could be embarrassed to be seen on an Order gathering with their partner, giving too much time and emphasis to something that 'wasn't spiritual'. Gatherings these days are much more relaxed, and people are more able to be themselves.

7) Learn to relate healthily to our teachers

Compared to Asia, Western culture has little in the way of prece-dents or models of how to relate to our spiritual teachers. We don't even have a word for our role in that relationship. By contrast, however, there is such a word in the Pali canon: *sekkha* ('one undergoing training').[142] Developing mature teacher-student relationships has been a painful process in many Western sanghas.

There is an inherent tension between thinking for ourselves and listening to our teacher. Especially when we are lacking personal experience of the spiritual life, we may respond by being naive, gullible, unquestioning, and conformist. Then we might go through a phase of rebellion and resentment, becoming disrespectful and individualistic. The mature response is a middle way between the two; we are able to be receptive and courteous, but also thoughtful and independent. Sometimes, we may decide – quite freely and individually – to do what our teacher suggests even if it is not what we'd rather do. We are willing to trust their experience and judgement.

The FWBO has also learned appropriate – and beautiful – ways to express the gratitude we may feel to our founder and teacher. On some recent Order gatherings I've been on, and during which Sangharakshita has been giving a talk or question-and-answer session, we've finished by chanting the White Tara mantra[143] for him. He has sat quietly receiving the 'blessing' of the mantra.

8) Realize our dependence on community

If we are realistic and honest about ourselves, most of us know we could not practise the spiritual life alone. Though times of solitude can be invaluable, we also depend on the spiritual community – on the teachings, inspiration, ethos, and exemplification that flow through it. The health and harmony of the sangha is therefore of the utmost importance.

The spiritually mature realize this and experience themselves as part of a community. We realize that each person is responsible for themselves, but that, in another way, we are responsible for one another too. We are therefore willing to operate on the basis of consensus and harmony, not necessarily going off and doing what we want to do, regardless of the consequences for the wider community.

9) Don't polarize over 'perennial issues'

In maintaining the integrity and life of a community, there are ongoing balancing acts. For example, there may be a tension between 'unity' (common, clearly defined practices that hold a community together) and 'diversity' (a more varied approach to practice that allows for individual differences). Another balancing act may be between 'growth' (spreading the Dharma through new centres and projects) and 'depth' (consolidation to ensure there is sufficient weight of practice).

There are no set answers to these tensions; they are balancing acts that require vigilance, reflection, and adjustments of approach over time. But we can get impatient, or by temperament we may incline a particular way, and so can polarize with other people who tend in the opposite direction. We need to learn to work with the contradictions, and maintain a creative balance.

The Order has learned much in this area too, setting up debates in a way that avoids polarization, allowing people to express their opinions freely, while staying in touch with a deeper harmony.

❧

This book has only been able to give a brief overview – to show just some of the highs and lows of the process by which a new Buddhist movement developed and grew. Behind that collective story are, of course, thousands of individual tales that could be told, stories of lives touched and transformed by the Dharma. Here are just a few.

In 1991 Carol Baillie, a single mum with three children, was living in Emerald, a small town in the Dandenong Ranges to the west of Melbourne, Australia. She managed to get to a weekend meditation retreat in Melbourne, but she knew she'd never be able to attend classes there more regularly. She asked the Order member who was running the weekend what she should do. His immediate reply was that if she could get a few people together in her lounge, he'd come and teach on a fortnightly basis. She was bowled over by the generosity of this response, and from someone she hardly knew. The Order member was Buddhadasa – the same Buddhadasa who had established the first FWBO centre at Archway in London almost 20 years before.

Within a few weeks Carol had 15 people in her living room and every fortnight Buddhadasa, accompanied by Manjusiddha, made the hour-and-a-half journey out of rush-hour Melbourne and up the mountain road to Emerald. Over the years, a sangha started to emerge. Some of that original group still attend, some are Mitras, and some have asked for ordination.

At one time, Buddhadasa was going to be away travelling, but he told Carol he was sure she could keep the class going while he was away. She didn't share his confidence. A few days before the first week of the new term of classes, a package arrived from the other side of the world. It was a beautiful Tibetan singing bowl. There was no covering letter or note, but Carol knew immediately, '… it was Buddhadasa's gift to me and it represented the transference of his confidence to my own heart. It is the most precious gift I have ever received.'[144]

Carol was ordained in 1999 and given the name Maitripala (which means 'protector of loving-kindness'). And the Buddhism and meditation classes continue at the Dandenong Ranges Buddhist Community.

❧

Ian Guthrie[145] had been a heroin addict for nine years. For the last six of those he'd financed his habit through burglary, and had been to prison twice. One Thursday night in 1986 he was lying in bed in utter distress and despair; he just couldn't face another day of heroin and crime. Suddenly, in the middle of the night – and he has no idea where it came from – he had the strong conviction that he needed to learn about Buddhism and meditation.

Friday, Saturday, and Sunday were the usual days of heroin, but on the Sunday night Ian walked past Croydon Buddhist Centre. He knew the place; he'd burgled it twice. A poster on the door advertised an 'Open Evening' on the Monday night. He went along.

Nothing spectacular happened, no amazing meditation experiences, but the people were warm and friendly and somehow he left the building with a new resolve to put heroin behind him. For the next two weeks, he went through 'cold turkey' while continuing to go along to classes at the Buddhist centre.

In the middle of those two weeks it suddenly hit him; he'd burgled these people who were trying to help him. The thought weighed on him terribly. Crying, he went straight out to the Buddhist centre and told two Order members, Padmaraja and Padmavajra, that he was the one who'd been burgling them. There was a silence and then one of them said, 'Good, good … it's good to meet someone so honest.' This forgiving response was almost unbearable; he had been expecting them to get angry and call the police. Later, Ian made arrangements with them to repay the money he had stolen.

Later, he wrote to Sangharakshita and told him this story. He received a reply, the last line of which read, 'With the help of spiritual friends, make up for lost time.' Ian was ordained in 1999 and received the name Lokamdhara, 'he who supports the world'.

Malati,[146] born in 1962, was one of a large family of 13 children, living with her parents, aunts, and uncles in a house in Pune, India. Ever since her grandfather – who had met Dr Ambedkar several times – had converted in the great mass conversion ceremony of 1956, the family had been Buddhist, and was well known in the Buddhist community.

When Lokamitra from London was starting Buddhist activities in Pune, he came to their family for help to find premises. They offered him a room in the house and, later, space in a nearby warehouse. The young Malati was fascinated to see a Westerner wearing robes. The monks in India didn't usually teach, but would just 'bless and go'. It felt special to have a foreigner come and actually teach them Buddhism and meditation.

After finishing her degree she got involved in TBMSG, first of all translating for Padmasuri, another Westerner. Her family had received several offers of marriage for her to wealthy young men, but she wanted to marry a Buddhist. Eventually, a marriage was arranged for her with Padmananda, an Indian Order member. It meant they could support each other in their Buddhist practice, bringing up their two children, but also giving each other 'time off' to go on retreat. She was ordained on 1 January 2003 and received the name Karunadipa.

Now Karunadipa is chairwoman of Bahujan Hitay Pune Project, which runs a whole array of social projects, largely funded by Karuna Trust. There is a crèche for children whose parents both have to work, medical facilities, five different sewing classes that give women a way to earn a livelihood, adult literacy classes, karate classes for 630 children that help them to develop confidence as well as physical fitness, other sports facilities, study classes where children from poor, overcrowded families can come and do their school homework each evening, and a savings group that helps families avoid borrowing money at high interest rates.

Karunadipa 'cried like anything' when she was ordained; she felt so happy and loved her name, which means 'lamp of compassion'.

❧

Simhacitta[147] was 76 and had lived for 12 years in Sarana men's community in Bristol, UK. The Bristol Buddhist Centre had recently moved into much bigger premises, but they'd been struggling with the mortgage repayments. At one stage there had even been talk of having to downsize again, which would have been immensely disheartening.

On the morning of 6 June 2003, Kevala discovered Simhacitta collapsed in his room and rushed him to hospital, where he died. Then they found he'd written a cheque the night before and left it on the mantelpiece of his room. It was for £5000, made payable to the Bristol Buddhist Centre. Why had he done that? They would never know for sure, though they learned later that he'd also left a substantial amount to them in his will. Once all the legalities were sorted out, they were able to pay off the bulk of their mortgage and so stay in the larger property.

Simhacitta was an amateur woodworker and had a collection of various pieces of wood. The community made his coffin from them, which was hand painted by various members of the sangha. The funeral at the Buddhist centre was a great celebration of his life, and a lesson to them all in how to die well.

❧

One hundred years ago, a substantial portion of humanity lived in cultures where Buddhism was a significant influence. Now it is in massive decline, repressed by the effects of Communism in places like China and Tibet, undermined by consumerism in places like Taiwan and Japan. According to Stephen Batchelor:

> Never in human history has such a major world religion diminished in size and influence so rapidly. Three or four revolutions in the right place would more or less eliminate traditional Buddhism from the face of the earth.[148]

While many of its branches are rapidly dying back, two regions where Buddhism is putting forth fresh new shoots are the post-industrial countries in Europe, the Americas, and Australasia, and in the Buddhist revival in India.

The FWBO is responsible for some of those shoots. It could continue to make a significant contribution and could even play a role in the regeneration of Buddhism in its traditional heart-lands.

Currently, the world can feel unsafe, threatened by global warming, the 'war against terrorism', or economic meltdown. It can seem like the human race is confronted by a stark choice between the forces of materialistic consumerism and religious fundamentalism. Buddhism has a vision of human life that would lend the material success of the West more depth and meaning. It upholds ethics and values without resorting to religious dogma. It has much to offer the modern world.

In the heady, early days, people thought the FWBO was going to change the world. Of course, it was naive, but what is the point of exchanging that belief for a cynical conviction that we can't change anything? We all create the world we live in through our actions. It always hangs in the balance. On one side are those actions which arise from greed, hatred, and unawareness; on the other side are those arising out of generosity, love, and wisdom. A community of people, working in harmony, and inspired by a common vision, *can* add significantly to the positive side of the scale.

This has been the story of the generosity, idealism, courage – and mistakes – of the many pioneers who created the FWBO. You learn what it is you are trying to do in the process of trying to do it. Much has been learned in the first 40 years. Now it is up to us what we make of it.

12
Postscript

I've been telling the story of the birth and growth of a spiritual community, one that is still developing and maturing. In other words, it is an unfinished story, one whose chapters are still unfolding. While most of this book was written in late 2008, the year that followed was a highly significant one for the FWBO. This postscript describes – rather briefly – developments up to the spring of 2010.

In the 'post-*Guardian*' era, there was much reappraisal of the FWBO's way of practising the Dharma. Long-standing members of the Order were asking themselves, after all those years of trying, whether it had really worked. Were they becoming happier, more content, more spiritually mature human beings? And could they find within the FWBO what they needed to take their spiritual practice further and deeper?

The questioning seemed to be accompanied by two main trends. First, there was a decline in the proportion of those who lived in communities or worked in team-based right livelihoods. Of the Order members who took part in the 2007 Order survey, 30% lived in a Buddhist community and 20% were employed in the FWBO. These were much smaller proportions than in the early days of the movement.[149]

Most people welcomed the increased diversity of lifestyle, and yet some also worried that a crucial and distinctive aspect of the FWBO's approach to the Dharma was endangered.[150] The movement didn't just offer a set of practices to do in the privacy of one's own life. The FWBO was a practice in itself: participation in the sangha required, and helped to develop, qualities of cooperativeness, generosity, and sharing that worked in opposition to the individualistic tendencies of contemporary consumer society. Communities and team-based right livelihood businesses could be ideal places to practise sangha in this way. They offered a different way of life. If fewer people participated in them, it would be a loss not only to those who wanted to live that way of life, but also to the intensity and effectiveness of the whole sangha.

A second trend occurred in the area of meditation practice. Perhaps the first four decades of the FWBO had primarily been about building a new movement. The creation of vibrant sangha, and the institutions that sustained it, had been paramount. Now, some people wondered if they needed something different. There was discussion about whether it was possible to attain 'stream entry'[151] or 'insight' in the FWBO. Some Order members went to other Buddhist teachers looking for personal tuition in meditation practice, especially in *satipatthana* meditation and in 'choiceless' or 'non-directed' meditation practices. A few of them started to bring what they had learned into the FWBO, some of them teaching new practices on retreats and at urban centres.

There was a sense of excitement and enthusiasm; discoveries were made that were genuinely helpful. No doubt there was a need for the FWBO to develop more detailed and nuanced teaching and exploration of meditation. Yet the bringing-in of new practices sometimes led to polarization between Order members. Those trying new approaches could be dismissive of the 'standard'

FWBO practices; people doing those 'standard' practices could be defensive and suspicious of anything new. There were times when new practices were brought in with little or no wider discussion. This could cause confusion when it resulted in different FWBO teachers advocating seemingly contradictory approaches.

All this provoked a discussion on the 'coherence' of the sangha. In April 2009 Sangharakshita published his own contribution to the debate. 'What is the Western Buddhist Order? A Message from Urgyen Sangharakshita' was sent to all Order members and to many other people in the FWBO worldwide.[152]

The paper began by exploring how new spiritual communities arise in the Buddhist tradition, based on the teaching and practices recommended by a founding figure:

> Every Sangha presupposes a Dharma: a particular Sangha presupposes a particular presentation of the Dharma ... the Dharma needs to be made specific to a particular Sangha. It needs to hang together, doctrinally and methodologically, if it is to be the basis of a Sangha or Order.[153]

Sangharakshita argued that there was a danger of mixing different approaches to the Dharma:

> For commitment to be strong it has, in a sense, to be narrow. It is only through intensity of commitment and practice that you achieve any results. You will not achieve that intensity if you try to follow different teachers and their different teachings and practices at the same time.[154]

Mixing too many different practices had implications for the unity and effectiveness of the sangha as well:

If everybody is doing different practices it becomes harder and harder to have a sense that we are one Order, as some people begin to feel more and more allegiance to the group of those who do their own particular form of practice. In addition, the more variety of practice there is, the harder it will be for people to find guidance in their practice from more experienced practitioners within the Order. We are a united spiritual community and so we need to keep a common body of practice, a common vocabulary of practice...[155]

Sangharakshita also restated his belief in the importance of the 'New Society' – of communities and team-based right livelihood projects that offered people a fully Buddhist way to live:

I feel the need to emphasize them more than ever … It's not enough for us to practise Right Livelihood as best we can out there in the world. The ideal work situation is Team-based Right Livelihood, where dana[156] is generated and spiritual friendship can be developed more intensively. I also still believe in the single-sex communities and other single-sex activities … they weren't just an adaptation to the circumstances of the sixties and seventies. They are of permanent value.[157]

He reiterated his confidence in the FWBO's path of practice:

I think that a few people are over-concerned with Stream Entry and Insight. In some cases the concern becomes almost neurotic: it seems to indicate a lack of faith in the Dharma and certainly a lack of faith in what we are practising. One should just be concerned about practising the Dharma to the full extent of one's ability, then Stream Entry will look after itself. And the average Order member has more than sufficient resources in terms of teachings, practices, and supportive institutions to gain Insight…. If you study the teachings that you have got from me, if you apply them systematically and regularly over a period of time, don't worry, the results will come.[158]

There was a range of responses within the Order. Some were relieved that Sangharakshita had spoken out. It seems likely that most were broadly happy with what he'd said. Others felt that their motives for going to other teachers had not been understood, or that the need for 'coherence' was now being overemphasized. That summer's European Order Convention was based on exploration of these themes, with 'conversation cafés' and panel discussions that allowed the five hundred or so people who attended to dialogue around the issues. Some had arrived at the Convention expecting difficulty and disagreement. However, it was remarkably harmonious for most people – a testament to the maturity of the Order and its ability to debate difficult issues.

The Order was learning how to balance 'unity' and 'diversity'. 'Unity' could lean over into being too rigid, and a sangha being unable to adapt to different temperaments or changing circumstances. But there was also a point at which 'diversity' could tip over into the sangha being too diffuse and fragmented. There was a perennial tension between the two, an ongoing balancing act. A spiritual community always walked a tightrope; on one side lay the danger of conservatism and conformity, and on the other confusion and incoherence. Sangharakshita was speaking out because he felt the Order had started to tilt too far one way and it was time to redress the balance.

The discussion will no doubt continue. There needs to be further exploration of the processes by which a large spiritual community ensures that practices and teachings are developed in harmony with the whole existing system of practice. There is also likely to be more discussion about meditation practice; for example a re-emphasis on the 'just sitting' element of Sangharakshita's system of meditation.[159]

❧

As the Order debated these issues throughout 2009, it became apparent that questions around Sangharakshita's sex life still lingered in the background. Some in the Order and FWBO remained troubled by his sexual activity in the past. They couldn't understand why he hadn't replied to the criticisms that had been made, and this led them into doubt in him and his teaching.

In the autumn of 2009, in conversation with two senior Order members (Mahamati and Subhuti), Sangharakshita spoke very openly and personally about his sexuality, remarkably so for a man well into his eighties. He was finally telling his side of the story of what had happened all those years ago when he'd become sexually active. He talked about the reasons for his previous reluctance to speak out, and the process by which he had changed from being a celibate monk to being sexually active, and about the effect of this on the development of the FWBO.[160]

Although Sangharakshita was never secretive at the time of his sexual relationships, he didn't say much about them after criticisms were made. He explained:

> I have always been very reticent and reserved. There are reasons for that in my early experience. First of all, from an early age I realized that my serious interests were not shared by anyone else I knew, so I

just did not talk about them. As time went on, that included my interest in the Dharma: there was no one in my immediate circle I could talk to about that. ... I think my general tendency has been not to disclose my deeper feelings or real thoughts. That has of course spilled over and reinforced my reluctance to talk about my sexuality.[161]

He talked about his experience of growing up in the 1930s and 1940s and realizing he was homosexual:

In all the recent discussions about me in this respect, to the best of my knowledge, no one seems to have considered what it must have been like for me, growing up at a time when all forms of homosexual activity were regarded as criminal. It could have had a much more unfortunate effect upon my character than it did. ... Nonetheless, although I was aware of society's disapproval, I did not disapprove of myself for having those inclinations.[162]

He was, however, celibate as a young man and then also when he became a Theravadin monk in India. He now spoke candidly about what that was like for him:

I won't say that I found celibacy easy. I don't think I am celibate by nature, so it was a definite struggle, but of course it was a struggle in which I believed at that time. I think probably the period of the greatest struggle was during my earlier years in Kalimpong, when I was between about 25 and 35. It was quite difficult remaining celibate during that period, although I did manage.[163]

He was aware that many other monks struggled, and many had sexual relationships 'on the quiet'. He also met several married Tibetan lamas and observed that they were impressive and committed practitioners. Gradually, over time, he began to inwardly question the emphasis given to the celibate monk's life.

Back in London in the late 1960s and 1970s, he found himself in an entirely different situation. Homosexuality had been decriminalized, sexual freedom was in the air, and eventually he had a sexual relationship with a young man named Carter:

> This period … was quite idyllic and very liberating for me, in tune with the mood of the times. It was the first time in my life that I had had an opportunity of this kind. I was of course also getting on with setting up the Movement: taking classes and so forth. The two aspects were very much intertwined and were both important to me. It was a very rich, fruitful, creative period and I had a lot of energy that expressed itself in all sorts of ways, including the sexual, as well as in Dharma talks, poetry, etc. Some of the things going on might have been seen as incompatible, but they were not, so far as I was concerned at the time. It all seemed right and natural.[164]

And so he ended up enjoying an active sex life. At the time it seemed very straightforward. His experience was one of being on a level with people, not of being the 'Teacher' from on high.

> I did not feel I was forcing anybody and would have regarded that as a quite wrong thing to do. … I was having sex because I was attracted to the person and saw, or thought I saw, an answering response.[165]

But, if in a very few cases there had been misunderstandings, he was sorry.

Since the late 1980s Sangharakshita has been celibate again: 'During this last phase, celibacy has come quite naturally and happily to me – it is the way I want to be.'[166]

In hindsight it wasn't ideal that the opportunity to explore his sexuality coincided with his founding of the FWBO: 'It would have been tidier if I'd got all that out of the way and sorted out, neatly and nicely, before I started the FWBO, but it couldn't be like that. I couldn't have waited till I was 75!'[167]

On the other hand, it all had positive implications for how Buddhism could be lived in the contemporary world. In a traditional Buddhist society, before the era of contraception and when homosexuality was taboo, there were only two options: the life of a celibate monk (which most seemed to find extremely difficult to accomplish healthily, without resorting to suppression of emotions) or family life (which for most people limited the time and energy they had available for Dharma practice and for helping to make the Dharma available to others).

But now other possibilities were opening up:

> My sexual activity was part of a wider process in my own personal life – and one might even say in my Dharma life and in my attempt to communicate the Dharma. It was part of a general exploration. I was trying to explore how to live and communicate the Dharma in these very new circumstances of the modern West. I had become aware that there were aspects of life that were being given a new kind of attention in modern culture – aspects of life that the Dharma had never previously had to address. I had to work out for myself how the Dharma related to these aspects of life, since there were no clear and

explicit models to be found in the scriptures or in traditional Buddhism.[168]

What resulted in the FWBO were 'semi-monastic' situations – living and working situations where it was possible to devote most of one's time to a fully Buddhist life, but also to have a sexual relationship. For example, one might live in a community but have a sexual relationship with someone living nearby, or in another town:

> What we have developed then is a broader range of possibilities for leading the spiritual life than has traditionally been found. ... It is possible now, at least in the West, to live without a family but without renouncing sex, at least until one is able to be happily celibate. Our semi-monastic institutions ... make this possible and are therefore a vital and unique contribution to the practice of the Dharma today.[169]

Both of these communications from Sangharakshita were important, clarifying the nature of an Order or spiritual community, and also trying to help people understand him and aspects of his past. In the first communication, the emphasis was on 'conserving' – maintaining a coherent, clear, consistent tradition. In the second, Sangharakshita was giving a sense of how, to some extent, the FWBO had arisen out of a willingness to experiment, to question the assumptions of Buddhist tradition or of the surrounding society, and of being prepared to be 'radical'. As the story of the FWBO continues into the future, this will be another of those perennial challenges: how both to conserve, keeping a common body of practices and common language, and also to remain radical, applying the message of the Dharma to changing times and situations.

A third – and surprise – communication came from Sanghar-akshita in early 2010. He wrote to all Order members strongly suggesting that the name of the Order be changed to 'Triratna Buddhist Order'. He also proposed that the FWBO should become the 'Friends of the Triratna Buddhist Order' but, in response to a request from chairs of Buddhist centres in Europe, accepted their alternative proposal of 'Triratna Buddhist Community'.

A change of name had long been debated in the movement, and now Sangharakshita was putting his weight behind a change. The fact was that the movement was no longer solely 'Western'. It had to be known by a different name in India, and the name 'Friends of the Western Buddhist Order' translated into very different forms in different languages. Because it was so long, it invari-ably got reduced to an acronym: 'FWBO' in English, 'AOBO' in French and Spanish, 'VWBO' in Dutch, and 'BBBD' in Turkish! These acronyms could be unwieldy and failed to communicate the meaning and character of the movement.

By changing the name to 'Triratna Buddhist Community', 'Triratna' for short, the movement would have one name world-wide. Having one name would promote unity and be a reminder of how all can go for refuge to the Three Jewels. 'Triratna' means 'Three Jewels' – the central ideals of Buddha, Dharma, and Sangha. Sangharakshita's teaching had always stressed that the Buddhism practised in his movement was about focusing on the core teachings of the tradition – ideals and practices summed up in the Three Jewels. Lastly, the name emphasizes friendship and community.

The proposal was vigorously debated. Some Order members in the West were sorry to lose the word 'Western' from the name; being known as 'Western Buddhists' was meaningful to them. However, a majority could see the need for one name worldwide, and so in Spring 2010, the names of the Order and movement were changed to 'Triratna Buddhist Order' and Triratna Buddhist

Community. In April 1967, in a tiny basement room in London, Sangharakshita inaugurated the Triratna Meditation Room and Shrine of the Friends of the Western Sangha. 43 years later, on Wesak (the festival of the Buddha's Enlightenment) in May 2010, Buddhist centres all over the world marked the change of the name from 'FWBO' to 'Triratna Buddhist Community'.

Works Cited and Referenced

Batchelor, Stephen. 1994. *The Awakening of the West: The Encounter of Buddhism and Western Culture*. London: Harper Collins.

Bunting, Madeleine. 1997. 'The Dark Side of Enlightenment'. *Guardian*, 27 October, G2 supplement, pp.1–4.

Burch, Vidyamala. 2008. *Living Well with Pain & Illness*. London: Piatkus Books.

Dayanandi. 1997. 'Building Tara's Realm: The Story of Taraloka Women's Retreat Centre'. In Kalyanavaca (ed.). *The Moon and Flowers: A Woman's Path to Enlightenment*. Birmingham: Windhorse Publications.

Dhammadinna. 1979. 'Why Single-Sex Communities?'. *FWBO Newsletter* 44 (Winter).

Dhammadinna. 1998. 'Sexual Evolution'. *Dharma Life* 8 (Summer); also at http://fwbodiscussion.blogspot.com/2007/07/sexual-evolution.html.

Dhammapada.

FWBO Communications Office. 1998. 'The FWBO-Files: A Response', August; also at http://response.fwbo.org/fwbo-files/response1.html.

FWBO Newsletter 18 (Spring 1973).

FWBO Newsletter 27 (Summer 1975).

FWBO Newsletter 46 (Summer 1980).

FWBO Newsletter 54 (Summer 1982).

The Gist, the newsletter of Glasgow FWBO, 2005.

Golden Drum 12 (February–April 1989).

Gross, Rita M. 1988. *Soaring and Settling: Buddhist Perspectives on Contemporary Social and Religious Issues*. New York: Continuum.

Gross, Rita M. 2001. 'Women in Buddhism'. In Peter Harvey (ed). *Buddhism*. London and New York: Continuum.

Karuna Trust Financial Report 2008.

Kornfield, Jack. 2002. *A Path with Heart: The Classic Guide Through the Perils and Promises of Spiritual Life*. Rider: London.

Kularatna. 1982. 'Setting Out'. *FWBO Newsletter* 54.

Mason-John, Valerie. 2008. *Broken Voices: 'Untouchable' Women Speak Out*. New Delhi: India Research Press.

Metcalf, Barbara D. and Thomas R. Metcalf. 2006. *A Concise History of Modern India*. Oxford: Oxford University Press.

Lokabandhu. 2007. The Order Survey: The Order's Relation with the FWBO, November, available at: http://freebuddhistaudio.com/ordersurvey.

Loy, David R. 2008. *Money, Sex, War, Karma: Notes for a Buddhist Revolution*. Boston: Wisdom Publications.

Madhyamavani 4 (Spring 2001).

The Middle Way. 1980. 55:3 (November), p.143.

Moksananda. 2001. 'Going Forth from Nationalism'. *Madhyamavani* 4 (Spring).

Nagabodhi. 1988. *Jai Bhim: Dispatches from a Peaceful Revolution*. Glasgow: Windhorse Publications.

Omvedt, Gail. 2004. *Ambedkar: Towards an Enlightened India*. New Delhi: Penguin Books India.

Padmasuri. 2002. *Transforming Work*. Birmingham: Windhorse Publications.

Padmavajra. 1988. 'Beginnings'. *Golden Drum* 10 (August–October).

Paramacitta. 2000. 'Bringing the Dharma to Spain'. *Lotus Realm* 14 (Autumn–Winter).

Parami. 1998. 'Sex, Power, and the Buddhist Community'. *Lotus Realm* 9 (Spring–Summer), pp.5–10.

Queen, Christopher S. 1996. 'Introduction: the Shapes and Sources of Engaged Buddhism'. In Christopher S. Queen and Sallie B. King (eds). *Engaged Buddhism: Buddhist Liberation Movements in Asia*. Albany: State University of New York Press.

Ratnaguna. 1995. *Discipleship in the Western Buddhist Order*. Surlingham: Padmaloka Books.

Ray, Reginald A. 1994. *Buddhist Saints in India: A Study in Buddhist Values and Orientations*. New York: Oxford University Press.

Sangharakshita. 1985. *The Eternal Legacy: An Introduction to the Canonical Literature of Buddhism*. London: Tharpa Publications (reissued in 2006 by Windhorse Publications).

Sangharakshita. 1986a. *Alternative Traditions*. Glasgow: Windhorse Publications.

Sangharakshita. 1986b. *Ambedkar and Buddhism*. Glasgow: Windhorse Publications.

Sangharakshita. 1988. *The History of My Going for Refuge*. Glasgow: Windhorse Publications.

Sangharakshita. 1990. *My Relation to the Order*. Birmingham: Windhorse Publications.

Sangharakshita. 1992a. *Buddhism and the West*. Glasgow: Windhorse Publications.

Sangharakshita. 1992b. *The Three Jewels: An Introduction to Buddhism*. Glasgow: Windhorse Publications.

Sangharakshita. 1994. 'Fifteen Points for Buddhist Parents', talk given at the

Works Cited and Referenced

London Buddhist Arts Centre, April; available on DVD from Clear Vision (http://www.clear-vision.org/Home-Use/FWBO-Videos/fwbo-DVDs/Sangharakshita-talks.aspx).

Sangharakshita. 1995. *Peace is a Fire*. Birmingham: Windhorse Publications.

Sangharakshita. 1996a. *Extending the Hand of Fellowship*. Birmingham: Windhorse Publications.

Sangharakshita. 1996b. *Great Buddhists of the Twentieth Century*. Birmingham: Windhorse Publications.

Sangharakshita. 1996c. *A Guide to the Buddhist Path*. Birmingham: Windhorse Publications

Sangharakshita. 1996d. *In the Sign of the Golden Wheel*. Birmingham: Windhorse Publications.

Sangharakshita. 1997. 'Looking Back – and Forward', talk at Birmingham Buddhist Centre, April; also available on DVD from Clear Vision (http://www.clear-vision.org).

Sangharakshita. 2001. *A Survey of Buddhism: Its Doctrines and Methods Through the Ages*, 9th revised edition. Birmingham: Windhorse Publications.

Sangharakshita. 2003. *Moving Against the Stream*. Birmingham: Windhorse Publications.

Sangharakshita. 2006. *In Retrospect*, DVD interview with Nagabodhi.

Sangharakshita. 2009. 'What is the Western Buddhist Order?' at http://www.sangharakshita.org/news.html, April (pdf).

Urgyen Sangharakshita (ed. Karen Stout). 2009. *The Essential Sangharakshita*. Boston: Wisdom Publications.

Sangharakshita (interviewed by Nagabodhi). 1987. 'Buddhism, Sex, and the Spiritual Life'. *Golden Drum* 6 (August–October).

Shabda. Various contributions.

Sponberg, Alan. 1996. 'TBMSG: A Dhamma Revolution in Contemporary India'. In Christopher S. Queen and Sallie B. King (eds). *Engaged Buddhism: Buddhist Liberation Movements in Asia*. Albany: State University of New York Press.

Sponberg, Alan. 1992. 'Attitudes to Women and the Feminine in Early Buddhism'. In Jose Ignatio Cabezon (ed). *Buddhism, Sexuality, and Gender*. Albany: State University of New York Press.

Srinivas, M.W. (ed.). 1996. *Caste: Its Twentieth Century Avatar*. New Delhi: Viking.

Stark, Rodney. 1996. 'Why Religious Movements Succeed or Fail'. *Journal of Contemporary Religion*, 11(2), pp.133–46.

Subhuti. 1994. *Sangharakshita: A New Voice in the Buddhist Tradition*. Birmingham: Windhorse Publications.

Subhuti. 1995a. *Bringing Buddhism to the West*. Birmingham: Windhorse Publications.

Subhuti. 1995b. *Women, Men, and Angels*. Birmingham: Windhorse Publications.

Subhuti. 1996. *Unity and Diversity: The Sangha Past, Present, and Future*. Surlingham: Padmaloka Books.

Subhuti. 2003. *Roads to Freedom*. Birmingham: Madhyamaloka.

Suvarnaprabha. 2008 (orig mid-1990s). 'Tearing Open the Dark: Inquiries into Being Female in the Friends of the Western Buddhist Order', at http://2golden.blogspot.com/search?q=inquiries+into+being+female.

Vidyamala. 2000. 'Being Here'. *Dharma Life* 14 (Winter), pp.16–19; also at http://breathworks-mindfulness.org.uk/resources/vidyamala-burch-being-here.html.

Vishvapani. 1998. 'Learning the Harsh Way'. *Dharma Life* 7 (Spring), pp.59–60; also at http://fwbodiscussion.blogspot.com/2007/02/learning-harsh-way-at-croydon-buddhist.html.

Vishvapani. 2001. 'Testing Articles of Faith'. *Dharma Life* 17 (Winter), p.48; also at http://www.dharmalife.com/issue17/testingfaith.html.

Vishvapani. 2004. Book review (Joseph Goldstein. *One Dharma: The Emerging Western Buddhism*), *Western Buddhist Review*, 4, at http://www.westernbuddhistreview.com.

Vishvapani. 2007. 'The Great Escape'. *Tricycle* (Spring, vol 16.3), at http://www.tricycle.com/feature/the-great-escape.

Watts, Nigel. 2003. *Writing a Novel*. London: Hodder Education.

Author's Private Correspondence and Interviews, *including with*
Siddhisambhava, January 2009.
Vidyamala, interview, Manchester Buddhist Centre, June 2009.

Online-only Sources
http://breathworks-mindfulness.org.uk
http://freebuddhistaudio.com
http://www.appeals.karuna.org
http://www.fwbo-files.com
http://www.fwbojhb.co.za
http://www.fwbomitracourse.com
http://www.inform.ac/infmain.html
http://www.karuna.org
http://www.windhorsepublications.com
http://www.wildmind.org

Works Cited and References

Hillman, James. 2001. 'Betrayal'. *Black Sun Journal,* at http://www.blacksunjournal.com/psychology/18_betrayal-part-1-of-3-by-james-hillman_2001.html.

Sangharakshita. 2002. 'Six Distinctive Emphases of the FWBO'. http://freebuddhistaudio.com/talks/details? num=197.

Sangharakshita. 2009a. 'Conversations with Bhante, August 2009', http://www.sangharakshita.org/interviews/CONVERSATIONS_AUGUST_2009.pdf.

Sangharakshita. 2009b. 'What is the Western Buddhist Order?', http://www.sangharakshita.org/What_is_the_Western_Buddhist_Order.pdf.

Subhuti. 2004. 'Where I Am Now' and 'Where I Want to Be', available to Western Buddhist Order members at http://freebuddhistaudio.com/.

Other Useful Sources

Suryaprabha. *History of the FWBO*, 4 films on the early history available for download at http://lightsinthesky.org.

Notes

1 Ursula Le Guin, quoted in Nigel Watts. 2003. *Writing a Novel*. London: Hodder Education, p.16.

2 Throughout the book, references to numbers of 'centres' means FWBO sanghas with their own dedicated premises. References to 'centres and groups' also include FWBO groups running in houses or rented rooms.

3 Sangharakshita. 1992a. *Buddhism and the West*. Glasgow: Windhorse Publications, p.8.

4 The Theravada is the school of Buddhism that predominates in countries such as Sri Lanka, Burma, and Thailand. There are two stages to ordination: the *sramanera* ('novice') ordination, which was given to Sangharakshita by U Chandramani in May 1949; and the full *bhikkhu* ('monk') ordination, which Sangharakshita received from U Kawinda in November 1950.

5 A *vihara* is a dwelling place for monks, where they can pursue and promote the study and practice of Buddhism. Sangharakshita's vihara was known as Triyana Vardhana Vihara, which means 'the place where the three yanas (the three main historical phases of Buddhism) flourish'.

6 Now in its ninth edition. Sangharakshita. 2001. *A Survey of Buddhism: Its Doctrines and Methods Through the Ages*. Birmingham: Windhorse Publications.

7 Sangharakshita. 1992b. *The Three Jewels: An Introduction to Buddhism*. Glasgow: Windhorse Publications; Sangharakshita. 1985. *The Eternal Legacy: An Introduction to the Canonical Literature of Buddhism*. London: Tharpa Publications (reissued in 2006 by Windhorse Publications).

8 The historical development of Buddhism is sometimes divided into three great stages: Hinayana, Mahayana, and Vajrayana, each with their own characteristic practices, emphases, and doctrinal developments. The Theravada is the sole remaining school of Hinayana Buddhism, while Tibetan Buddhism combines Mahayana and Vajrayana.

9 You can read Sangharakshita's account of this conflict, and also of his friendship with Terry Delamere, in his 2003 volume of memoirs, *Moving Against the Stream*. Birmingham: Windhorse Publications.

10 A year later, after the first ordinations into the Western Buddhist Order, and after a debate in which some people had said they wanted a name that didn't contain words like 'sangha' that would sound unfamiliar to newcomers, the movement changed its name to Friends of the Western

Notes

Buddhist Order (FWBO).

11   Sangharakshita. 1997. 'Looking Back – and Forward', talk at Birmingham Buddhist Centre, April; also available on DVD from Clear Vision (http://www.clear-vision.org).

12   *FWBO Newsletter* 18 (Spring 1973), p.5.

13   In addition to the historical Buddha (known as Shakyamuni), the later Buddhist traditions of the Mahayana and Vajrayana recognize numerous archetypal Buddhas and Bodhisattvas. Each has his or her own iconography, myths, and symbolism, and embodies a particular aspect of Buddhahood. Avalokitesvara is one such archetypal Bodhisattva; he embodies and expresses the compassion of Enlightenment.

14   *FWBO Newsletter* 27 (Summer 1975), centre pull-out section.

15   A 'Buddhaland' is a realm created by the compassionate activity of a Buddha, where there are the ideal conditions for practising the Dharma and attaining Enlightenment.

16   If you want to explore the seminars, many FWBO centres will have paper transcripts of them in their libraries. They give a sense of the history and early culture of the FWBO, as well as imparting information about the Dharma. The transcripts are also archived at http://free-buddhistaudio.com/texts/seminars and Windhorse Publications has edited a number of them into book form.

17   'Bhante' is a term from the Theravada tradition for respectfully addressing one's teacher.

18   Subhuti. 2003. *Roads to Freedom*. Birmingham: Madhyamaloka, p.35.

19   Sangharakshita. 2006. *In Retrospect*, DVD interview with Nagabodhi.

20   Reprinted in *The Gist*, the newsletter of Glasgow FWBO, in 2005.

21   'Metta' is often translated as 'loving-kindness'.

22   Interview in *Women's Own*, 23 September 1987; see: http://www.margaretthatcher.org/speeches/displaydocument.asp?docid=106689.

23   *The Middle Way*. 1980. 55:3 (November), p.143.

24   Vishvapani. 2004. Book review (Joseph Goldstein. *One Dharma: The Emerging Western Buddhism*), *Western Buddhist Review*, 4, at http://www.westernbuddhistreview.com.

25   Sangharakshita. 1995. *Peace is a Fire*. Birmingham: Windhorse Publications, p.79.

26   *FWBO Newsletter* 54 (Summer 1982), p.19.

27   Vishvapani. 1998. 'Learning the Harsh Way'. *Dharma Life* 7 (Spring), pp.59–60; also at http://fwbodiscussion.blogspot.com/2007/02/learning-harsh-way-at-croydon-buddhist.html.

28   See Chapter 3 for an explanation of becoming a Mitra.

29   Author's interview with Manjunatha, July 2009.

30   *Golden Drum* 12 (February–April 1989), p.24.

31   Nagabodhi. 1988. *Jai Bhim: Dispatches from a Peaceful Revolution.* Glasgow: Windhorse Publications, p.34.

32   For more on how caste operates, see MW Srinivas (ed.). 1996. *Caste: Its Twentieth Century Avatar.* New Delhi: Viking, especially pp.4–5. To read personal stories of how caste affects the lives of women in India today, plus some general information on caste, see Valerie Mason-John. 2008. *Broken Voices: 'Untouchable' Women Speak Out.* New Delhi: India Research Press.

33   To read more about the life and work of Ambedkar, see Sangharakshita. 1986b. *Ambedkar and Buddhism.* Glasgow: Windhorse Publications, and Gail Omvedt. 2004. *Ambedkar: Towards an Enlightened India.* New Delhi: Penguin Books India.

34   Quoted in Omvedt 2004, p.135.

35   Quoted in Omvedt 2004, p.61.

36   Quoted in Vishvapani. 2007. 'The Great Escape'. *Tricycle* (Spring), p.117.

37   A note on terminology: *Dalit* means 'oppressed' and is the word by which 'ex-Untouchable' peoples have often referred to themselves. *Harijan* ('children of God') was a term coined by Gandhi and often used in India to refer to 'ex-Untouchables'. The 'ex-Untouchables', however, consider it patronizing and do not use the term. 'Scheduled castes' is another term, and refers to the fact that India's new constitution provided a quota of places in higher education and in government service to people from the oppressed communities. However, many of those who have converted to Buddhism refer to themselves solely and simply as Buddhists, leaving behind any identification of themselves in relation to the caste system. From now on in the text, I will use the term 'Dalit', unless referring specifically to those who have converted to Buddhism, in which case I'll use terms such as 'new Buddhists' or 'Ambedkarite Buddhists'.

38   See note 4.

39   This extraordinary event is described in Sangharakshita. 1996d. *In the Sign of the Golden Wheel.* Birmingham: Windhorse Publications, Chapter 23.

40   Sangharakshita 1996d, p.342.

41   Lokamitra. 2008. 'Thirty Years in India'. *Shabda* (private newsletter of WBO/TBM) (August).

42   *Dhamma* is the Pali equivalent for the Sanskrit word *Dharma* – the Buddhist path, teaching, or truth. In the Indian wing of the movement,

Notes

the Pali term is usually used, so I will use that term from now on in this chapter.

43 Kularatna. 1982. 'Setting Out', *FWBO Newsletter* 54, p.8.

44 The 'three worlds' refers to the three worlds of traditional Buddhist cosmology (*karmaloka*, *rupaloka*, and *arupaloka*), and also to the first, second, and third worlds of modern geopolitics.

45 In India, the Order was known as the 'Trailokya Bauddha Mahasangha' (TBM).

46 Padmavajra. 1988. 'Beginnings', *Golden Drum* 10 (August–October), p.9.

47 Karuna means 'compassion'. You can find out more about the work of the Karuna Trust at http://www.karuna.org.

48 Stephen Batchelor. 1994. *The Awakening of the West: The Encounter of Buddhism and Western Culture*. London: Harper Collins, p.365.

49 If you are interested in taking part in an appeal, contact Karuna Trust via their appeals website at http://www.appeals.karuna.org.

50 Alan Sponberg. 1996. 'TBMSG: A Dhamma Revolution in Contemporary India'. In Christopher S. Queen and Sallie B. King (eds). *Engaged Buddhism: Buddhist Liberation Movements in Asia*. Albany: State University of New York Press, p. 101.

51 Karuna Trust Financial Report 2008, p.2.

52 The first three 'challenges' I list are from Sponberg 1996, pp.105–10.

53 Sangharakshita. 1996b. *Great Buddhists of the Twentieth Century*. Birmingham: Windhorse Publications, p.26.

54 Sangharakshita. 1988. *The History of My Going for Refuge*. Glasgow: Windhorse Publications, p.117.

55 Christopher S. Queen. 1996. 'Introduction: the Shapes and Sources of Engaged Buddhism'. In Christopher S. Queen and Sallie B. King (eds). *Engaged Buddhism: Buddhist Liberation Movements in Asia*. Albany: State University of New York Press, p.46.

56 Sponberg 1996, p.76.

57 Sangharakshita 1996b, p.26.

58 *FWBO Newsletter* 46 (Summer 1980), p.27.

59 For more on the story of Windhorse:Evolution, see Padmasuri. 2002. *Transforming Work*. Birmingham: Windhorse Publications.

60 In this context, 'right livelihood' means using your work and working context as a means to spiritual transformation, as well as to be cultivating ethical and expansive states of mind during the working day.

61 Sangharakshita. 2002. 'Six Distinctive Emphases of the FWBO', http://freebuddhistaudio.com/talks/details? num=197.

62 Author information from Windhorse:Evolution, early 2008.

63   Vidyamala Burch. 2000. 'Being Here'. *Dharma Life* 14 (Winter), pp.16–
      19; also at http://breathworks-mindfulness.org.uk/resources/vidyamala-
      burch-being-here.html.

64   This quote and later ones are from the author's interview with Vidyamala
      at the Manchester Buddhist Centre, June 2009.

65   For more on Breathworks™, see http://breathworks-mindfulness.org.uk.

66   Vidyamala Burch. 2008. *Living Well with Pain & Illness*. London:
      Piatkus Books.

67   This principle is discussed further in Chapter 8.

68   Sangharakshita. 1994. 'Fifteen Points for Buddhist Parents', talk given
      at the London Buddhist Arts Centre, April; available on DVD from
      Clear Vision (http://www.clear-vision.org/Home-Use/FWBO-Videos/
      fwbo-DVDs/Sangharakshita-talks.aspx).

69   Reginald A. Ray. 1994. *Buddhist Saints in India: A Study in Buddhist
      Values and Orientations*. New York: Oxford University Press.

70   Subhuti. 1996. *Unity and Diversity: The Sangha Past, Present, and Future*.
      Surlingham: Padmaloka Books.

71   Lokabandhu. 2007. The Order Survey: The Order's Relation with the
      FWBO, November, pp.6, 10 (available at: http://freebuddhistaudio.
      com/ordersurvey). One-third of the Order outside India – i.e. 400
      Order members – took part in the survey.

72   Dhammadinna. 1979. 'Why Single-Sex Communities?'. *FWBO News-
      letter* 44 (Winter), p.6.

73   Ibid, p.7.

74   Ibid, p.7.

75   Lokabandhu 2007, p.3.

76   Dayanandi. 1997. 'Building Tara's Realm: The Story of Taraloka Women's
      Retreat Centre'. In Kalyanavaca (ed.). *The Moon and Flowers: A Woman's
      Path to Enlightenment*, Birmingham: Windhorse Publications.

77   Akasaraja. 2004. In *Shabda* (privately published WBO/TBM news-
      letter), May, at http://fwbodiscussion.blogspot.com/2007/07/seven-
      years-experience-of-working-at.html.

78   Vishvapani 1998, p.61.

79   Subhuti. 1995b. *Women, Men, and Angels*. Birmingham: Windhorse
      Publications.

80   Subhuti. 1994. *Sangharakshita: A New Voice in the Buddhist Tradi-
      tion*. Birmingham: Windhorse Publications, p.168. As Subhuti states,
      however, there are different views and interpretations of what Buddhist
      tradition says on this topic. For more on attitudes to women in Buddhist
      tradition, see Rita M. Gross. 2001. 'Women in Buddhism'. In Peter
      Harvey (ed). Buddhism. London and New York: Continuum, pp.205ff.,

Notes

and Alan Sponberg. 1992. 'Attitudes to Women and the Feminine in Early Buddhism'. In Jose Ignatio Cabezon (ed). *Buddhism, Sexuality, and Gender*. Albany: State University of New York Press, pp.3ff.

81   Sangharakshita has recently reiterated this point. He regards disagreement by an Order member with him on the issue of the relative spiritual aptitudes of men and women '… as a difference of opinion that does not affect their discipleship…. In addition, even supposing that women had less spiritual aptitude than men, at least in the early stages of the spiritual life, the whole weight of current popular opinion is so strongly against such a view that it would be wise not to insist on it, since it is not critical to someone's practice of the Dharma, and one doesn't want to discourage anybody without a good reason…. It is worth saying also that an Order member is not obliged to believe that men and women are exactly equal in their spiritual aptitudes.' See Sangharakshita. 2009. 'What is the Western Buddhist Order?' at http://sangharakshita.org/news.html, April, p.9 (pdf).

82   Subhuti 1995b, p.32.

83   Subhuti. 2003. in *Shabda* (privately published WBO/TBM newsletter), June, p.45 .

84   Lokabandhu 2007, p.19. Approximately 10% of women agreed with *Women, Men, and Angels*, 15% were 'not sure', and 75% disagreed. Of the men, approximately 25% agreed, 35% were 'not sure', and 40% disagreed.

85   Varadakini. 2008. 'Setting up FWBO Paris'. *Shabda* (privately published WBO/TBM newsletter), November, p.53.

86   Paramacitta. 2000. 'Bringing the Dharma to Spain'. *Lotus Realm* 14 (Autumn–Winter), p.18.

87   Moksananda. 2001. 'Going Forth from Nationalism'. *Madhyamavani*, 4 (Spring), p.75.

88   Paramacitta 2000, p.19.

89   Paramacitta 2000, pp.16–19.

90   For more about the Johannesburg Centre, see http://www.fwbojhb.co.za.

91   Suvarnaprabha. 2008 (orig mid-1990s). 'Tearing Open the Dark: Inquiries into Being Female in the Friends of the Western Buddhist Order', p.3, at http://2golden.blogspot.com/search?q=inquiries+into+being+female.

92   See Chapter 6 for a discussion of this issue.

93   Suvarnaprabha 2008, p.4.

94   Suvarnaprabha 2008, p.14.

95   See Chapter 3 for more detail.

96   Here, a kesa is a strip of white cloth, embroidered with symbols of the

Three Jewels (the Buddha, Dharma, and Sangha) worn by members of the Western Buddhist Order when teaching and on ceremonial or ritual occasions.

97 The refuges and ten precepts are verses of commitment to the Buddhist ideals of Buddha, Dharma, and Sangha, and ten ethical trainings.

98 Buddhist ordinations in Asia have often been monastic, although there are ordinations in Pure Land, Chan, Zen and Shingon Buddhism, for example, which are not exclusively monastic or celibate traditions.

99 Once an ordination lineage dies out, it cannot be revived. Full Buddhist monastic ordination for women is now available in China, Taiwan, Korea, and Vietnam, and possibly elsewhere in Asia, and even these lineages are not universally accepted as valid. In other Buddhist countries, women often live and practice as nuns, though they only have the 'novice' ordination, and therefore often receive less support and have lower status than the men monastics. See Gross 2001.

100 It is important to be clear that it is not the monastic lifestyle that is being criticized, but the *over-identification* of this as being synonymous with a true Buddhist spiritual life, and the undervaluing of other Buddhist lifestyles that may be equally committed and effective.

101 'Tantric initiation' is the giving of a special mantra and meditation practice in the Vajrayana Buddhist tradition. It is important to realize that Bodhisattva vows or Tantric initiations are not being criticized in themselves. They may be spiritually highly significant and meaningful. What is being criticised is the perception of them as spiritually superior to other forms, or expressions, of Going for Refuge.

102 For example, see Sangharakshita. 1996a. *Extending the Hand of Fellowship*. Birmingham: Windhorse Publications.

103 *Dhammapada*, verses 168, 169.

104 Sangharakshita 1988.

105 Sangharakshita 1988, pp.90–1.

106 Sangharakshita 1988, p.93.

107 Saccanama. 2009, in *Shabda* (privately published WBO/TBM newsletter), April, p.24.

108 Quoted in Sangharakshita. 1990. *My Relation to the Order*. Birmingham: Windhorse Publications, p.8.

109 Sangharakshita 1990, p.6.

110 Rodney Stark. 1996. 'Why Religious Movements Succeed or Fail'. *Journal of Contemporary Religion*, 11(2), pp.133–46.

111 Subhuti. 1995a. *Bringing Buddhism to the West*. Birmingham: Windhorse Publications; 1994. *Sangharakshita: A New Voice in the Buddhist Tradition*. Birmingham: Windhorse Publications.

Notes

112　Vishvapani. 2001. 'Testing Articles of Faith'. *Dharma Life* 17 (Winter), p.48; also at http://www.dharmalife.com/issue17/testingfaith.html.

113　Madeleine Bunting. 1997. 'The Dark Side of Enlightenment'. *Guardian*, 27 October, G2 supplement, pp.1–5.

114　To find out more about INFORM, see http://www.inform.ac/infmain. html.

115　Vishvapani 2001, pp.48–9.

116　See http://www.fwbo-files.com.

117　FWBO Communications Office. 1998. 'The FWBO-Files: A Response', August; also at http://response.fwbo.org/fwbo-files/response1.html.

118　Transcripts of Sangharakshita's and Subhuti's speeches were printed in *Madhyamavani* 4, Spring 2001.

119　Subhuti. 2003. in *Shabda*, March (privately published WBO/TBM newsletter).

120　Siddhisambhava, private correspondence with the author, January 2009.

121　For an interesting and useful discussion of sex and relationships in Western Buddhism by non-FWBO authors practising in the Zen and Tibetan traditions respectively, see David R. Loy. 2008. *Money, Sex, War, Karma: Notes for a Buddhist Revolution*. Boston: Wisdom Publications, and Rita M. Gross. 1988. *Soaring and Settling: Buddhist Perspectives on Contemporary Social and Religious Issues*. New York: Continuum.

122　For a helpful discussion of the FWBO's experimental approach to sex and relationships, see Dhammadinna. 1998. 'Sexual Evolution'. *Dharma Life* 8 (Summer), pp.28–31; also at http://fwbodiscussion.blogspot. com/2007/07/sexual-evolution.html.

123　'Mandala', in this context, means the overall pattern or structure of your life. The slogan was reminding people of the need to keep the ideals of Buddha, Dharma, and Sangha central in their lives, with other aspects of life seen in relationship to those ideals. See, for example, Sangharak-shita 1995, p.66: 'In the FWBO we do not have a puritanical attitude towards sex, but at the same time it must be recognised … that its place is at the periphery rather than the centre of our existence. Nowadays people tend to "over-invest" in the sexual-romantic type of relationship, with the result that their emotional balance is constantly being threat-ened and peace of mind becomes impossible of achievement.'

124　Sangharakshita. 1986a. *Alternative Traditions*. Glasgow: Windhorse Publications, p.180.

125　Clause 28 (more accurately, Section 28) was a 1988 amendment to the UK government's Local Government Act 1986 which prohibited local authorities from 'promoting homosexuality'. It provoked huge oppo-sition from the gay community and their supporters. The clause was revoked in 2003 (2000 in Scotland).

126   Dhammadinna 1998, p.28.

127   Sangharakshita (interviewed by Nagabodhi). 1987. 'Buddhism, Sex, and the Spiritual Life'. *Golden Drum* 6 (August–October), p.12.

128   Sangharakshita 1987, p.13.

129   For one public discussion of the issues in an FWBO magazine, see Parami. 1998. 'Sex, Power, and the Buddhist Community'. *Lotus Realm* 9 (Spring–Summer), pp.5–10.

130   Dhammadinna 1998, p.31.

131   Vipassi. 2003. 'Crisis or Critical Moment?. in *Shabda* (privately published WBO/TBM newsletter), May, p.14; also at: http://fwbodis-cussion.blogspot.com/2007/04/vipassi-crisis-or-critical-moment.html.

132   Sangharakshita 1990, pp.27–9.

133   Subhuti. 2003. in *Shabda* (privately published WBO/TBM newsletter), June, p.46 .

134   Subhuti. 2004. 'Where I Am Now' and 'Where I Want to Be', two talks given at Padmaloka to an audience of members of the Western Buddhist Order. The talks are available to Order members via http://freebuddhis-taudio.com/.

135   http://freebuddhistaudio.com.

136   http://www.fwbomitracourse.com.

137   http://www.wildmind.org.

138   Urgyen Sangharakshita (ed. Karen Stout). 2009. *The Essential Sanghar-akshita*. Boston: Wisdom Publications.

139   One of the inspirations for my summary of 'lessons learned' is the chapter on 'spiritual maturity' in Jack Kornfield's well-known book, *A Path with Heart*, although my emphases, and the language I use are different. Jack Kornfield. 2002. *A Path with Heart: The Classic Guide Through the Perils and Promises of Spiritual Life*. Rider: London, pp. 309–21.

140   James Hillman. 2001. 'Betrayal'. *Black Sun Journal,* at http://www.blacksunjournal.com/psychology/18_betrayal-part-1-of-3-by-james-hillman_2001.html.

141   Sangharakshita 1995, p.39.

142   Ratnaguna. 1995. *Discipleship in the Western Buddhist Order*. Surl-ingham: Padmaloka Books, p. 3.

143   Mantras are chants that generally have no conceptual meaning but express or evoke in sound the qualities of a particular Buddha or Bodhisattva figure. The White Tara mantra is traditionally chanted for a teacher or anyone for whom you wish long life, merit, and wisdom.

144   Related in personal email to the author, October 2008.

Notes

145 The following is based on a telephone interview with the author, April 2009.

146 The following is based on an interview with the author, August 2009.

147 The following is based on an interview of Saccanama, with the author, April 2008.

148 Quoted in Sangharakshita 1996a, p.17.

149 Lokabandhu 2007, pp.8, 13.

150 Respondents to the 2007 Order survey agreed overwhelmingly about the importance of 'positive institutions'. However, less than half saw the movement as 'building the new society': Lokabandhu 2007, p.18.

151 'Stream entry' is a traditional Buddhist term for describing a decisive turning point in the spiritual path. It is the point at which 'insight' – a direct seeing into reality – becomes irreversibly present in the practitioner. From then on, he or she is guided by that deeper spiritual vision or perspective.

152 Sangharakshita. 2009b. 'What is the Western Buddhist Order?', http://www.sangharakshita.org/What_is_the_Western_Buddhist_Order.pdf

153 Sangharakshita 2009b, p.4.

154 Sangharakshita 2009b, p.3.

155 Sangharakshita 2009b, p.18.

156 'Dana' is the Sanskrit word for 'generosity' or 'giving'. In this context, it refers to the fact that those who worked in team-based right livelihood projects generated profits that were crucial in funding Buddhist activities and spreading the Dharma.

157 Sangharakshita 2009b, p.23.

158 Sangharakshita 2009b, p.22

159 For an overview of the 'system of meditation', including a basic explanation of the idea of 'just sitting', see Sangharakshita. 1996. *A Guide to the Buddhist Path*, Birmingham: Windhorse Publications, pp.145ff.

160 Sangharakshita. 2009a. 'Conversations with Bhante, August 2009', http://www.sangharakshita.org/interviews/CONVERSATIONS_AUGUST_2009.pdf.

161 Sangharakshita 2009a, p.6.

162 Sangharakshita 2009a, p.7.

163 Sangharakshita 2009a, p.9.

164 Sangharakshita 2009a, pp.21–2.

165 Sangharakshita 2009a, pp.24, 27.

166 Sangharakshita 2009a, p.11.

167 Sangharakshita 2009a, p.32.

168 Sangharakshita 2009a, p.28,

169 Sangharakshita 2009a, p.44.

Index

About Windhorse Publications

Windhorse Publications is a Buddhist publishing house, staffed by practising Buddhists. We place great emphasis on producing books of high quality, accessible and relevant to those interested in Buddhism at whatever level. Drawing on the whole range of the Buddhist tradition, our books include translations of traditional texts, commentaries, books that make links with Western culture and ways of life, biographies of Buddhists, and works on meditation.

As a charitable institution we welcome donations to help us continue our work. We also welcome manuscripts on aspects of Buddhism or meditation. To join our email list, place an order, or request a catalogue please visit our website at www.windhorsepublications.com or contact:

Windhorse Publications Ltd.
169 Mill Road
Cambridge
CB1 3AN
UK

Perseus Distribution
1094 Flex Drive
Jackson TN 38301
USA

Windhorse Books
PO Box 574
Newtown NSW 2042
Australia

About Triratna

Windhorse Publications is an arm of Triratna Buddhist Community, which has more than sixty centres on five continents. Through these centres, members of Triratna Buddhist Order offer regular programmes of events for the general public and for more experienced students. These include meditation classes, public talks, study on Buddhist themes and texts, and bodywork classes such as t'ai chi, yoga, and massage. Triratna also runs several retreat centres and the Karuna Trust, a fundraising charity that supports social welfare projects in the slums and villages of Southern Asia.

Many Triratna centres have residential spiritual communities and ethical businesses associated with them. Arts activities are encouraged too, as is the development of strong bonds of friendship between people who share the same ideals. In this way Triratna is developing a unique approach to Buddhism, not simply as a set of techniques, but as a creatively directed way of life for people living in the modern world.

If you would like more information about Triratna please look for us on the Web or write to:

London Buddhist Centre
51 Roman Road
London E2 0HU
UK

Aryaloka
14 Heartwood Circle
Newmarket NH 03857
USA

Sydney Buddhist Centre
24 Enmore Road
Sydney NSW 2042
Australia

By the same author

Buddhism:
Tools for Living Your Life

by Vajragupta

Buddhism: Tools for Living Your Life is a guide for those seeking a meaningful spiritual path in busy – and often hectic – lives. An experienced teacher of Buddhism and meditation, Vajragupta provides clear explanations of the main Buddhist teachings, as well as a variety of exercises designed to help readers develop or deepen their practice.

ISBN 9781 899579 74 7
£10.99 / $16.95 / €16.95
192 pages